Astrology for Teens

Understanding Your Relationship to the Universe

By: Discover Press

Table of Contents

Preface

So, do you want to learn about Astrology and have no idea where to start? In this guide, we break down the basics: the planets, what they mean for you, and what to do when things get hard. Life is a roller coaster, and astrology can help you to make sense of it all. Plus, we will chat about puberty, menstruation, fighting with parents, and how astrology plays a role in every aspect of your life. It's never too early to start learning about what the stars have in store for you!

We will break down your chart, which is essentially where all the planets were at the time of your birth, and what that *really means*. It may sound like a lot of information, but don't worry—we are walking you through the very basics, so you can have an initial understanding. Astrology is so much more than your daily horoscope or your sun sign (which you probably know already...or do you, really?).

Arguably, the perfect time to start studying astrology is when you're a teenager. You're developing and creating your life, learning new things, and becoming yourself. Astrology will help you to better understand what becoming "you" really means and help you identify parts of yourself you never knew before. If you're ready to dive in and learn all about yourself and what the universe has in store for you, keep reading. You won't regret it.

The Big Three

If you have ever looked into astrology, you have probably heard the term "your big three." The big three consist of your Sun, Moon, and Rising (or Ascendant) signs which are huge indicators of your personality. This can sound kind of daunting as you are first looking into astrological patterns and your chart, but if you take anything away from this guide, it's to study the heck out of your big three. These astrological signs will create the foundation of your chart and, in essence, who you are. Plus, when you look through other people's charts, you'll start to see their big three in them as well, which will help you to understand *why they are the way they are*. Don't stress—we will break everything down for you. Buckle up; we are in for a ride!

Part I: Sun Signs

You are so much more than your sun sign.

It's true. Your sun sign is probably the sign that you already know and vibe with. It's based on where the Sun was the day you were born. So, if your birthday is February 28th, for example, you would be a Pisces. If you were born on Halloween, you're most definitely a Scorpio. This is Googleable, sure, but we've got it broken down for you here:

Aries: March 21 ~ April 19
Taurus: April 20 ~ May 20
Gemini: May 21 ~ June 20
Cancer: June 21 ~ July 22
Leo: July 23 ~ August 22
Virgo: August 23 ~ September 22
Libra: September 23 ~ October 22
Scorpio: October 23 ~ November 21
Sagittarius: November 22 ~ December 21
Capricorn: December 22 ~ January 19
Aquarius: January 20 ~ February 18
Pisces: February 19 ~ March 20

As you can see, the astrological year starts in the Aries season and ends with Pisces. Whatever day you were born is the most definitive indicator of your sun sign and the one sign that gets the most hype because it's the one most people know. While you are so much more than just your sun sign (yes, we will die on that hill), your sun sign is one of the most important signs for you to understand.

Why?

Your sun sign is the most basic foundation of who you are. The sun sign tells us our <u>life purpose and our style</u>; that's why people with the same sun signs often have similar personalities. Your sun sign is primarily based on the day you were born, but if you were born on a transition day into a new Zodiac season, you may have to check your birth time to find that out. (There will be more of an explanation about birth times when we get to your rising sign, don't panic!)

Regardless, you need to know the depth of your sun sign to understand the depth of who you are.

Think of your sun sign as the leader in your chart; it knows what's up, where to guide you, and what's best for you. The more you know about your sun sign, the happier life you will live. You may notice the striking similarities in other people who share your sun sign; from how they dress to what their interests are, there is an umbrella of overarching personality traits that will be similar for sun signs. Since the sun sign is the backbone of who you are, it's important to know some of the key traits to look out for to better understand how to live your life.

Here's a quick breakdown of some traits of your sun sign:

Aries: The Ram. People with Aries as their sun sign are usually impulsive, strong-willed, and embrace change like it's the only constant (which it is). Aries suns love to have fun, change their minds constantly, and breathe happiness into their lives and the lives of others. They are a fire sign (more on elements to come!), and the youngest of the Zodiac, inviting inspiration and passion everywhere they go. Aries love a challenge and are often leaders that are fiercely independent change makers.

What to watch out for: impulsivity, irritability, and being overly independent.

Taurus: The Bull. If you have Taurus as your sun sign, you live a life of luxury. A Taurus loves nothing more than to curl up on the couch with the new cashmere blanket they just bought, eat good food, and watch movies until the cows come home. Taurus suns make great parents, as they love to spoil those that they love while also staying grounded in their own opinions. Taureans are earth signs and love to love.

What to watch out for: stubbornness and overspending.

Gemini: The Twins. Gemini suns wake up each morning a different person. No, really. Geminis love to reinvent themselves and see things from multiple points of view. They love to download all kinds of new info and express themselves accordingly. Gemini is an air sign and is one of the most adaptable signs of the Zodiac.

What to watch out for: fatigue, overworking, and busyness.

Cancer: The Crab. If your sun sign is in Cancer, you probably find yourself to be very intuitive and emotional. Cancers are water signs, ruled by the Moon, and are very in touch with their emotions. A Cancer can pick up on the emotions of others, as well, and find themselves to be extremely empathetic. Cancers are usually taken with animals and surround themselves with furry friends. Similar to Taurus, Cancers love all things cozy, too.

What to watch out for: oversensitivity and codependence.

Leo: The Lion. Humans with Leo as their sun sign radiate sunshine and confidence everywhere they go. Leos are fire signs, ruled by the Sun, and are always the ones to take things to the next level. Don't be fooled, though: Leos are also very in touch with their emotions and are not scared to let you know. They light up every room they walk into and are often very honest with those they love.

What to watch out for: selfishness, self-centeredness, and bragging too much.

Virgo: The Virgin. If your sun sign is in Virgo, you are probably a very studious and organized individual. Virgos love to have everything put together; neat and tidy is the name of the Virgo game. Because of this, Virgos can be focused and career-centered. Virgos are an earth sign and remain grounded and put together even during complete chaos.

What to watch out for: reclusiveness, over-organizing, and obsessing.

Libra: The Scales. Libras are all about balance. As an air sign, they are fairly adaptable with whichever way the wind blows. Libras love style, fashion, and shopping (in a good way!). You'll find Libras to be the center of attention, while also being calming and loving at the same time. You know when a Libra walks into the room (think Kim K.).

What to watch out for: overspending and selfishness.

Scorpio: The Scorpion. If your sun sign is in Scorpio, you are probably innately creative and moody, while also balancing being the life of the party. Scorpios are the bad boys (or girls) of the Zodiac; they love to have fun, but also to be introspective and reclusive. A walking contradiction, Scorpios are one of the deep water signs.

What to watch out for: holding things in and being too blunt.

Sagittarius: The Archer. Speaking of the life of the party, Sagittarius humans are exactly that. A fire sign, Sagittarius people love to have fun, often acting on impulse. However, a Sagittarius person loves to learn new things, and Sagittarians are always open to trying just about anything once. They are arguably the funniest of the Zodiac, too.

What to watch out for: impulsivity and stubbornness.

Capricorn: The Sea Goat. Work, work, work; that's the name of the Capricorn game. As an earth sign, Capricorns are generally pretty grounded people. Whatever they are working on is always of the utmost importance, and they are strategic in their planning to complete their checklist. A Capricorn loves nothing more than a strict deadline and reward system for getting things done.

What to watch out for: not leaving enough time for fun and self-care.

Aquarius: The Water Bearer. Despite what you may think, Aquarius is not a water sign—it's an air sign. Aquas are the most unique of the Zodiac because they march to the beat of their own drum. They love what they love and are not worried about what others think about that. Aquarians have individualistic passions that set them apart from the crowd, and they like it that way.

What to watch out for: lack of emotion.

Pisces: The Fishes. Pisces are the oldest and wisest of the Zodiac. You will find Pisces to be very creative and introspective people—often inherently psychic, as their intuition runs wild. People that have Pisces as their sun sign will live their lives in a dreamlike state. As a water sign, Pisces are extremely in touch with their emotions and love to love.

What to watch out for: indecisiveness and lack of attention.

Well, there you have it. That was a quick run-down of the sun signs and why they are important. Although, you are so much more than just your sun sign. So, since you have the foundation of who you are, it's time now to continue our journey and see what other facets of your chart make you into the person you are destined to be.

Part Two: Moon Signs

Let's get emotional, shall we?

Have you ever heard someone say the phrase "the Moon and the tides," or that the Moon controls the tides? You were probably at the beach when you heard this and didn't think about it too hard. That's okay! The point here is that the Moon controls, well, the tides in the ocean. What we're getting at here is that your moon placement in your chart is how you emotionally react in your internal and external world. The Moon reveals our most intimate selves—the part of yourself that few rarely get to see.

The Moon shows us how we react in situations, highlights our habits, and explains to us why we instinctively do that thing every time that another thing happens. Your moon sign is where the Moon was at the time you were born and is going to be fairly unique to you. As the Moon moves quickly, it flows through the Zodiac cycle. So even though you may have the same sun sign as your BFF, you most likely have a different moon sign. That explains why you act so differently, doesn't it? Think about it like this: the Moon controls our emotions, but also how we take care of ourselves and those around us.

Because of the profound impact that the Moon has on your emotional state, it lands a spot in your big three, despite being a moon connected to Earth and not an individual planet. Your moon sign controls your tides, a.k.a. the inner workings of how you are and how you react to situations in your life. The Moon is often associated with parenting, as well, since parents can be very emotional about their children. Thus, understanding your moon sign, especially as a teen, is pivotal to understanding how you react to your parents. On the flip side, knowing your parents' moon sign can tell you a lot about why they parent the way they do and help you create a more cohesive relationship with them. (More on that later.)

If it gets overwhelming or confusing, think of your sun sign and moon sign as best friends (or lovers) that work together to create the magical combination that is you. Just like for your sun sign, we will break down all of the Zodiac signs and what it means if you have that sign as your moon sign. Don't worry, we have got you covered.

Here is a breakdown of some traits that you have when your moon sign is in these Zodiac placements:

Aries: An Aries moon thrives on getting what they want. There is a sense of urgency for those with this placement, and that can manifest as impatience. Aries thrive on impulsivity and change, but with the watery energy of the Moon, this can create an imbalance for an Aries moon. Aries are all about passion, and this creates a fiery placement as a moon sign—you will be passionate about everything all at once, and may find yourself a part of many different passion projects. Aries moons are defensive, and they can often take things pretty personally. However, their independence sets them apart from the crowd; they are not scared of putting themselves out there, and that confidence is truly unmatched.

What to watch out for: impulsivity, lashing out, taking on too much at once, and excessive independence.

Taurus: A person with their moon in Taurus is going to love all things routine. They crave the familiar and often won't be super receptive to change. A Taurus moon is very cozy, and people often find themselves at ease around this placement. Taurus moons are grounded and offer a sense of safety and nurturing to those they love. Once a Taurus moon has committed, they are unwavering; you will find them to be defensive of themselves and those they care for. Taurus moon people are often romantic, as they love to take care of their partners and give gifts as well.

What to watch out for: stubbornness, conservative thinking/closed-mindedness, and defensiveness.

Gemini: If you have Gemini as your moon sign, you are probably the funny one in your friend group. Gemini moons love to have a fun time and are usually pretty enjoyable to be around. Geminis love constant change, including within their home. So it's not uncommon to find them changing things up around their home, keeping it fresh and the vibes good. Gemini moons are often restless and create major shifts and changes in their lives taking on new projects effortlessly. While Gemini moons do often worry a lot, they channel that stress into works of art, spreading laughter wherever they go.

What to watch out for: obsessive tendencies, overworking, and anxiety/worry.

Cancer: Cancer is ruled by the Moon, which means that the Moon finds its home here in this sign. Thus, Cancer moons have extremely heightened emotions and can be extremely empathetic toward others as well. Cancer moons often live inside their heads; they are attached to the past and to what comforts them (think: friends, family, home, etc.). They love to be safe and feel comfortable while also being in tune with their emotions and surroundings. Cancer moons crave peace and harmony.

What to watch out for: oversensitivity and being self-absorbed.

Leo: Leo suns are known for being extremely extroverted and the center of attention; however, with Leo as a moon sign, this may manifest a little differently. Instead, Leo moons will be drawn to being in the spotlight only when they are comfortable. If a Leo moon is around their family and friends, they will lead any conversation. Humans with a Leo moon also like to bring out the light in those they love, often helping to create change for them.

What to watch out for: being controlling, dominating conversations, and selfishness.

Virgo: A person with a Virgo moon craves all things security. Virgo moons like to have everything in order, meaning that they are happiest when the bills are paid and the house is clean. A Virgo moon is your go-to for keeping things organized; they love a steady routine! Virgo moons over-worry if their environments are shaken, but they are often determined and can pull themselves back up. If a Virgo moon is appreciated, they appreciate you back!

What to watch out for: obsessiveness and anxiety.

Libra: Libra moons crave love and closeness with others. You will find that Libra moons are always in a relationship and feel safest when comforted by someone else. Libra moons enjoy socializing and are often the center of attention without meaning to be. They love to love, and that's okay because they make great friends and partners. If you're a Libra moon, you probably love to debate and have lively conversations, as that's what fuels your passion.

What to watch out for: excessive pickiness and fear of being alone.

Scorpio: Scorpio moons are known for being one of the most intense moon placements. That's because they crave emotional intensity; they want to be all-in 100% of the time. If you do something halfway, or without emotion, that will not fly for a Scorpio moon. They crave drama and will give their attention fully to it, as that's where a Scorpio moon feels most at home. Thus, a Scorpio moon is great to have in your corner because they love so intensely and have a fierce loyalty about them.

What to watch out for: too much intensity, obsessiveness, and defensiveness.

Sagittarius: Sagittarius moons crave freedom and personal space. As long as they are not locked up or cornered, they will thrive! Sagittarius suns love to learn, but in a moon placement, they love to teach. Since they are always learning and trying new things, a Sagittarius moon will want to take you along for the ride. Sag moons shy away from routine and would rather be spontaneous with everything in life.

What to watch out for: bossiness, recklessness, and impulsivity.

Capricorn: Capricorns love to work, and a Cap moon is no exception. They tend to be cool, calm, and collected. Capricorn moons hide their emotions under the surface, and instead try to spark joy in those around them. They love a routine and solid work ethic, and as such, a Capricorn moon will stay grounded and get all of their stuff done in the most efficient way possible. They love to plan, and they take charge of any trips or excursions you may go on!

What to watch out for: overworking and exhaustion.

Aquarius: Aquarius moons are the shy observers. Usually introverted, those with Aquarius as their moon sign will develop a tendency to analyze others. They are constantly taking in new information and wanting to get to know others around them. However, Aquarius often has a hard time with introspection and as such can be emotionally distant. So, if you have Aquarius as your moon sign, you could feel a little unbalanced. Aquarius moons are uniquely their own, which is why they love to find out what makes others unique, too.

What to watch out for: being closed off and emotionally distant.

Pisces: People who have Pisces as their moon sign are the most intuitive of the Zodiac. Thus, they are fueled by passion and emotion and can pick up on how others are feeling as well. A Pisces moon feels pretty homey with moon energy and uses their emotions to help others feel at home, too. While Pisces are often super dreamy and in their own world, those with a Pisces moon will feel an urge to help others, and they make great listeners to boot.

What to watch out for: absentmindedness and forgetfulness.

So, do you feel like you understand your moon sign and the emotions that surround you? That was all the details on your moon sign. The Sun tells you who you are; the Moon tells you *how* you are. But what about how other people see you? That is all up to your ascendent sign, also known as your rising sign.

Part Three: Rising Signs

What vibes do I give off?

Your rising sign is based on your exact birth time. Getting this information can be a little stressful, but there are some simple places you can start your search. To find your birth time, check your birth certificate if it's available (or get a copy from a records service), ask your family, contact the hospital where you were born, or see if there is a baby book or family album that contains it. However, if you can't find your birth time (some birth certificates do not have it recorded, or maybe you don't have a birth certificate) you can do a couple of different things:

Guess! See what your parents say and roughly estimate your birth time. It may not be exact, making it a different sign entirely, but at least you would have something to go on. Once you have a rough idea, read the descriptions below and see which sign you think fits best (you can also get others' opinions, since the rising sign is about how others see you!).

Ignore it completely! You also have the option to quite literally opt-out of a rising sign, if you so wish. You can still do a lot of work within your chart without it; however, your rising sign is your chart ruler (more on that later) and without it, you do miss a piece of the puzzle. It's ultimately up to you!

Once you have your birth time locked down or have decided what works best for you, you are now ready to dive into all things rising signs. Your rising sign is how you present to other people and answers the question, "How does the world see me?" Thus, your rising sign is also your *chart ruler* and says more about you than most of your other placements. Each Zodiac sign is ruled by a particular planet, and as such, so are you. The planet that your rising sign falls into becomes the one that rules you and the one you may find the deepest connection with. (We'd like to point out that the Sun and Moon are also considered "planets" in this sense; meaning they do rule over Leo and Cancer rather than a planet.) Think about it like this: the rising sign is the mask you wear when you meet someone new for the first time. Rising signs are important because they do a lot of heavy lifting as far as your overall chart is concerned, which is why they have a place in your big three.

Without further ado, let's jump into what each rising sign means, and what it means for you. Here's a breakdown of the traits of each rising sign:

Aries: An Aries rising likes to get things done. Not a lot of planning involved, but not impulsive either. Rather, Aries risings charge ahead. A human that has Aries as their rising sign will not be very patient, but always finds the most efficient way to do something. Taking action is the name of the Aries rising game.

What to watch out for: competitiveness and putting too much pressure on themselves.

Taurus: Taurus risings like to take their time. They crave stability and are not usually ones for change. However, Taurus risings will be fiercely loyal and always want the best for those that they love. Someone with a Taurus rising will be very cautious, and probably the "mom" of the friend group. Security is Taurus rising's bread and butter.

What to watch out for: not being very open-minded.

Gemini: Like a Sagittarius sun, a Gemini rising will be a forever student. Gemini risings love to learn and are constantly taking in the world around them with fresh eyes. A person who has a Gemini rising will always be asking questions, wanting to learn from the people around them, and taking in new perspectives they may not have thought of before. A Gemini rising will love to talk, and they are often just as clever as they are hilarious.

What to watch out for: being easily distracted and overwhelmed with information.

Cancer: Cancers, by design, are gentle people. They love to love, and when Cancer is in a rising sign, they will often feel very familiar. A Cancer rising will walk through life caring a little bit too much about those they love, while also offering a softness to the world that it truly needs. Cancer risings are the girl/guy/person next door who just wants to make you happy.

What to watch out for: getting easily overwhelmed or easily flustered.

Leo: Leo risings light up the room as they walk in. They simply cannot help but be the center of attention, even when they don't want to be. Humans with a Leo rising carry themselves as if they are performing; they often talk a lot and become the conversation carriers. While a Leo rising has a presence that is often noticed, they are not self-absorbed.

Rather, they simply notice what they look like to others and pay attention to it.

What to watch out for: being too self-conscious and overestimating themselves.

Virgo: Understated is the vibe of a Virgo rising. They are often shy humans, who take their time as they process each decision they make. A Virgo rising is often underestimated due to their understated personality, but they are extremely intelligent people who can rise to the top. A person with Virgo as their rising sign is slow and steady and looks methodically for guidance on what to do next.

What to watch out for: pickiness and being judgmental.

Libra: Libra risings tend to attract anyone and everyone to them. Humans with a Libra rising love to love and never stay single for long. They are nice, simple, and often fair, which helps maintain balance in the lives of their loved ones. Libra risings like to keep the peace, often helping others to restore their equilibrium. They want everyone to be happy and try to find the outcome of a situation that will make that happen.

What to watch out for: people-pleasing and indecisiveness.

Scorpio: Scorpio risings command the room; their vibe is always loud, even when they are not. A human with a Scorpio rising is likely to be extremely determined and have powerful energy about them. They encourage others to be strong, and they can look right through people to see them for who they are. Scorpio risings have an intensity that hardly goes unnoticed.

What to watch out for: coming on too strong.

Sagittarius: A Sagittarius rising is a sucker for fun. They love adventure, impulsive trips, and are always positive. Hopeful is a Sag rising's middle name, and they tend to inspire others they are around to be more positive. As a result, a Sagittarius rising will seek only the happy things in life and encourage others to do the same.

What to watch out for: impulsiveness and being overly opinionated.

Capricorn: Capricorn risings are the most serious of the Zodiac. However, they are also hilarious, if you can take a deadpan kind of comedy. As the resident comedian, Capricorn risings like to use their critical thinking of the world around them and turn it into something playful. Therefore, they are hard workers but take life at face value.

What to watch out for: harsh tones and bluntness.

Aquarius: We have said it before and we will say it again: Aquarians are the most unique of the Zodiac, and an Aqua rising is no exception. Aquarius risings have a personality that is all their own, and they love flaunting it. Aquarius risings are studious—they always want to learn and are curious about how others think. They are totally and completely themselves 24/7, and they appreciate when others accept them as such.

What to watch out for: selfishness and being standoffish.

Pisces: Pisces risings love to go with the flow. They don't have a plan (or even a "pla" for that matter) and often find themselves drifting through life. You never know who you might meet when you talk to a Pisces rising because they are a little bit different every day. They don't like labels or structure, and instead spend most of their time dreaming about their next big adventure.

What to watch out for: indecisiveness.

Well, there you have it. Do you feel like you understand your rising sign just a little bit more? Your big three signs do piece together the core of who you are, and if you don't read any further, you can put those signs to good use. However, your astrological makeup is so, so much more than just your sun sign or your big three. Eight other planets make up your chart, and that unique magic that makes you, you. Are you ready?

Other Planets

Woohoo! You've made it. Now that you understand your big three, it's time to delve into just what your other planets mean for your natal chart. By now, you understand a lot of the key characteristics of each sign and how they work. Pisces are dreamy, Taureans are stubborn, Sagittarians are here for a fun time. You get it. So, when you are looking at this list of other planets and what sign they are in your chart, you can take those traits of each sign and compare and contrast it with each planet.

For example, Cancer is by far the most in tune with their emotions of anyone in the Zodiac. Venus is the planet of love and controls how we love. If Venus is in Cancer, then you probably love your friends, family, and significant others in a very emotional way, and in turn, react strongly when your feelings are hurt. Cross-reference what you know about each Zodiac sign with each planet and how they contribute to your whole self, and everything will start to make sense.

Without further ado, let's jump into those other groovy planets and what they mean.

Mercury: Mercury is the planet of communication, and it rules over Gemini and Virgo. This planet represents intellect, reasoning, and pretty much anything that goes on in the rational mind. A person's ability to communicate with others and their general communication style is ruled by their

Mercury sign. If you have any difficulties with communication, Mercury is often to blame. Mercury is where your mind breaks up thoughts and feelings, pushing the feelings off to your moon sign and rationalizing your thoughts.

Venus: Venus is the planet of love, and it rules over Taurus and Libra. This planet represents the power of attraction, how we love and seek partners, and how that manifests on a physical or spiritual level. Venus rules over what we value—from money, to love, to our self-worth and well-being. Whatever your core values are, they probably stem from your Venus sign and how that Zodiac sign interprets things you hold dear. How you spend your money and how you love others and yourself are what Venus rules over most.

Mars: Mars is the planet of desire and rules over Aries. This planet represents action, achievement, and independence and describes how you take initiative. Mars cares about how we take action and if we are assertive enough to meet our goals and get what we want. Mars is the opposite of Venus, and instead of tapping into emotion, Mars charges ahead and works to get things done. Mars helps you to realize what you want in life and works to help you achieve it. Whatever you desire can be yours—at least according to Mars, anyway.

Jupiter: Jupiter is the planet of human expansion and rules over Sagittarius. This planet focuses on human expansion in the physical, material, and spiritual world. Whichever sign Jupiter is in tells you how this experience will occur in your life. How you grow entirely depends on your Jupiter sign, especially as you move forward into future careers or life purposes. Growth in all areas of your life is possible with Jupiter by your side.

Saturn: Saturn is the planet of restriction, limitation, and maturity, and it rules over Capricorn. Saturn is often thought of as a difficult planet, but it truly provides structure to your life and guides your transition into adulthood. The sign that Saturn falls under in your chart tells you how you experience energetic blocks in your life and how you structure your agenda. Whatever your fears, limitations, and responsibilities are is revealed throughout your Saturn placement in your chart. When Saturn eventually does return to the same position in which you were born—usually around age 27 to 30—you will enter into astrological adulthood (but more on that later.).

Uranus: Uranus is the planet of evolution and rules over Aquarius. This planet represents freedom and breaking away from the norm. The sign where Uranus lies in your chart tells you how you will do this—how you will break through societal and self-imposed norms to show the world who you are. Uranus helps you discover your true self and drives self-evolution in mysterious and unpredictable ways. What makes you different is what makes you beautiful, and Uranus will always remind you of that.

Neptune: Neptune is the planet of inspiration and rules over Pisces. This planet represents inspiration, idealism, and spiritualism. Neptune tells you how you work to develop your spirituality. In your chart, everyone in your generation will share your Neptune sign, meaning that you will find like-minded people who share your spiritual beliefs. Neptune is a bit dreamy, and as such, it allows for you to always dream bigger and work to achieve those inspirations.

Pluto: Pluto is the planet of transformation and rules over Scorpio. This planet represents death, transformation, and power. The sign where Pluto resides in your chart shows you how you exercise your power of leadership and how you utilize transformation. Every time a cycle ends in your life, Pluto is there to catch you and transform you into the person you're destined to be. Don't worry, this little planet always has your back.

It is important to keep in mind that most of these planets do not need your initial birth time. So, if you do not have your birth time, do not fret. Most of these planets will be correct for you regardless. However, if you were born on a day where the planets shifted from one sign to the next, it is imperative to try to get as close to a birth time as you possibly can. A quick online search will tell you if a planet shifted to a new sign on your birthday, and if it did, try to track down your birth time! But a lot of these planets take years to rotate to a new sign, which is why planets like Neptune stay in same sign for entire generations.

Each planet tells you a little about who you are—from how you handle situations and what your values are to what you want to do with your life. Now, you do not have to have anything figured out at this moment, of course. But trust that everything is written in the stars for you. As you begin to figure out who you are, the planets are helping you on your journey. If you struggle in relationships, that's okay—maybe check in with your Venus sign and see why. If you're not sure what you want to do with your life yet, do not worry; Neptune and Pluto have you covered. If you're ever bullied for being different, trust that Uranus made you different because one day it will be the thing that makes you shine. You are exactly where you need to be at this moment, on your way to who you will be.

Do you feel that you have a better grasp on the planets now? Awesome! See, that was not so scary. You can now break down your big three and the rest of the planets that make you who you are. Did you know that each Zodiac sign has one of the four elements (Earth, Air, Fire, or Water) assigned to it, too? Up next, we break down each of the elements so you can understand even more about each Zodiac sign, and maybe why you are drawn to certain elements yourself.

The Elements

Now that you have a grasp on the planets, Zodiac signs, and how they behave and influence each other, it's time to understand what's going down here on Earth. Each Zodiac sign has its own element assigned to it, and those elements also explain even more about the characteristics of each sign. These elements are Earth, Fire, Air, and Water.

You'll find that you may be drawn to certain elements, and always have been, and that they could be the predominant element in your chart! Most of us have all the elements throughout our charts, but not always. You may have a lot of one specific element in your chart, which is common. If you're a *stellium* (which means that you have more than three placements in the same Zodiac sign), you'll have an abundance of that sign's element as well. You may be drawn to that element or find that its characteristics ring true for you. Whatever the case may be, these four elements hold a lot of weight as far as astrology is concerned. Ready to learn about them?

Earth Signs (Taurus, Capricorn, Virgo): People who have earth signs in any placement are considered to be very grounded. You'll find that Taureans tend to be more ethereal, lazy, and big spenders. Capricorns are hard workers that are often headstrong. Virgos can be overwhelmed easily but are very put together at the same time. Drawing from the Earth's energy, earth signs bring us back to the center. They enjoy all the gifts that Mother Nature provides, but also stay completely grounded in everything they do.

Fire Signs (Sagittarius, Leo, Aries): If you have a fire sign in your chart, you are probably impulsive and love to have a good time, to some extent. While Aries are more stubborn and set in their ways, Sagittarius loves to party and have the most fun one could ever dream about. Leos are the confidence masters, lighting up every room they walk in. Fire sign energy reminds us to always be a kid; anything can be fun if you choose to make it so. Drawing on fiery energy, fire signs will always lead you toward happiness and a good time.

Air Signs (Gemini, Libra, Aquarius): People that have air signs in their charts are the most adaptable people in the Zodiac. All of the air signs are extremely unique and cannot ever fit into one box. Geminis are new people every day and love to learn, Aquarians are uniquely themselves all the time, and Libras love to love and provide balance to others. Carrying air energy everywhere they go, air signs are blowing through life with change being the only constant.

Water Signs (Pisces, Cancer, Scorpio): Water sign people are very in tune with their emotions. If you have a lot of water signs in your chart, your emotions are as deep and impactful as the ocean. Cancers love deep emotional connections and find comfort in others, Pisces are intuitive and use their emotions to grow, and Scorpios thrive on mystery and are the life of the party. Swimming through their watery, dreamy energy, water signs spread calming energy anywhere their tides may take them.

While the four elements can seem pretty self-explanatory, there is much more to them underneath the surface. Because of the specific planets being in different Zodiac signs on the day you were born, they could have positive or negative relationships with that sign, depending on the planet that rules it. That's kind of confusing, we know. Here's an example:

If you have a Cancer moon, your moon sign will feel right at home, as it is in domicile. This essentially means that Cancer is in its ruler, the Moon. With the Moon ruling Cancer, you shouldn't have any friction. Cancer is a water sign and the most emotional of the Zodiac, fitting perfectly into the moon sign category.

However, if you have an Aries Venus, you may find that you are a little conflicted. Aries is ruled by Mars, Venus' opposite. So, if your Venus is in Aries, it is in detriment; detriment meaning that Mars is the ruler of Aries, being Venus' direct opposite. Thus, you may struggle to understand how you love and want to receive love. Aries is a fire sign, and Venus rules over Taurus and Libra (earth and air signs, respectively), which are directly conflicting energy.

If you have a sign in detriment like an Aries Venus, do not fret. That does not mean anything is inherently wrong with you or that it is not a "good" placement. All that means is that you may feel conflicting energy when researching that part of your chart. This may indicate an area of your life that may need extra time and attention. It will act as a lifelong challenge. Continuing with the Aries Venus example, even though Aries is in detriment in a Venus placement, Aries people are still capable of loving and being loved. They love affection and flattery and love others with passion and eagerness. While misunderstood often, an Aries Venus is still an incredible placement, despite its discomfort within its opposite planet. Does that make sense?

In the last section, we talked about all the planets and their ruling signs. Therefore, when you look at the elements of each sign, you can see how they interact with your planet's placements. In that vein, let's dissect this chart to give you a better idea of how the elements, Zodiac signs, and planets interact:

Sun in Pisces	♓	
Moon in Cancer	♋	
Mercury in Aquarius	♒	
Venus in Aries	♈	
Mars in Pisces	♓	
Jupiter in Capricorn	♑	
Saturn in Pisces	♓	
Uranus in Aquarius	♒	
Neptune in Capricorn	♑	
Pluto in Sagittarius	♐	
Rising Sign in Leo	♌	

This chart was created by the app, Horos.

As you can see, there are a lot of planets and conflicting energies at play here. For example, their moon

31

sign is in domicile in Cancer, but their Venus and Neptune signs are in detriment. There's a Pisces stellium, with Mars, Saturn, and the Sun all in Pisces. Add to that rising in Leo, and you have a very fiery water sign person, mixed with a small bit of earth and air as well. It is common to have every element represented in your natal chart; however, this person may feel an abundance of water throughout theirs. That being said, they are probably intuitive and emotional, but passionate and social with the conflicting fire signs, a logical thinker with the Capricorn and Aquarius signs, and so on.

You can see now how the elements impact each Zodiac sign, and since each sign has a ruling planet, those planets are also impacted by the elements, too. Rather, the person with the conflicting elemental energy (or lack thereof) is directly affected by each element. Either they feel more of one element than another, or an even combination of each to make up who they truly are. If you find yourself drawn to running in the grass or swimming, maybe you have a lot of earth or water placements. Love sitting by the fire or flying in an airplane? That's fire and air, baby.

One last thing that is important to note about the elements: They do have an opposite. Such is life! Here's how it works:

Water is opposite Fire
Air is opposite Earth

With that in mind, you may find yourself in conflict with others whose primary elements oppose yours. Water signs are more reserved and introverted, while fire signs are passionate, impulsive, and extroverted. Air signs are introspective and logical, and earth signs are pushers and hard workers. Water and fire signs tend to attract each other, while air and earth signs are often drawn to each other. It's a cliche for a reason: *opposites attract.* That doesn't mean that you cannot be friends with your opposing sign! Instead, it's to help you understand why they did that super annoying thing last Tuesday, *and* why it was annoying to you.

At the base level, the elements are pretty much what you probably already know them to be. So when you are looking through your chart, look at each planet and their Zodiac sign, and cross-reference what element that Zodiac sign is in and what Zodiac sign that planet is ruled by. Then you can start to better understand that special blend of goodness that makes your chart yours.

Modalities of Zodiac Signs

You may be looking at the title of this section and saying, "huh?" What in the world is a modality, and why should you care? Don't worry, we are going to break it down for you.

Astrology is so much more than just your horoscope. As you have gone through these sections, you can see that astrology and the Zodiac is quite complex. However, we are not here to overwhelm you with info; rather, we're just giving you the basics instead. Enter: Modalities.

Modalities are the *three major categories* in which your earth, fire, air, and water Zodiac signs are put into. Think about it like this: each of the twelve Zodiac signs is ruled by a specific element, but some of them have more in common than others. Modalities group together signs of different elements and highlight what they have in common, which helps you to deepen your understanding of each sign. Cross-reference the modalities with your chart, and you can really delve deep into who you are!

If you are looking to go a little bit deeper now that you understand the basics of how everything works, we have got you covered.

Without further ado, let's jump right into modalities!

The three modalities highlight the unique ways in which each Zodiac sign expresses their individuality and energy, how they react to given situations, and how they move through the world and operate in life. *Modalities are not the same as Elements*; rather, they are a different way of grouping the Zodiac signs based on personality traits.

The three modalities are: Cardinal, Fixed, and Mutable signs.

Everything you need to know about Cardinal Signs:

The cardinal signs are: *Aries, Capricorn, Libra, and Cancer*. Cardinal signs are important and create a foundation for themselves and others. You will often find cardinal signs in leadership positions, as they like to take charge. All four of the cardinal signs represent the beginning of a new season, and they love to be the ones who start new projects. The cardinal signs pave the way for new things. Likewise, cardinal natives are visionaries, and even though it can take them a hot minute to decide what those visions are, you can trust them to kick things off. Cardinal signs bring enthusiasm and passion in all that they do.

Everything you need to know about Fixed Signs:

The fixed signs are: *Taurus, Leo, Scorpio, and Aquarius*. Fixed signs are the Zodiac members who love to get things done. They want to help, and while they may not always be leaders, they are doers. Out of all of the signs, fixed signs understand the importance of steady and consistent work. They are the work horses of the Zodiac. That said, fixed signs have their eye *fixed* on their goals and aspirations, and nothing will get in the way of them. Once a fixed sign has their mind set on something, nothing can stand in the way. Fixed signs come along in the exact middle of each season, acting as a stabilizing force within the Zodiac cycle. Fixed signs are the man (and woman) with a plan and often can find their worlds disrupted without one. However, you can always rely on a fixed sign to get the job done.

Everything you need to know about Mutable Signs:

The mutable signs are: *Gemini, Virgo, Sagittarius, and Pisces.* Mutable signs are the final modality. Think of Mutable signs as the cherry on top: the final piece of the puzzle that ties everything into a nice, neat bow. Mutable signs are extremely flexible and can adapt to any situation with ease. They understand change very well and have no problem incorporating it into their lives. Mutable signs are able to go with the flow. They understand that with every negative encounter they have, a positive one always comes along to balance it. Mutable signs are able to understand multiple different perspectives, acting as the peacekeepers of the Zodiac. These signs love to help others find positive endings to any negative situation, and because of that, they can help others be okay with change, too.

Modalities are not that difficult to understand, especially when you have a grasp on the signs, your big three, and their elements, too. If you think about what you've learned so far, then everything will start to make sense about how the modalities are grouped, even if you just think about them as signs throughout each season of the year. You get the idea!

Menstruation Station

So, for this section, we are going to talk about the intersection between menstruation and astrology. Particularly, we'll examine the overlap with the cycles of the Moon and your own moon sign! If you are not a person that has a period, feel free to move ahead (or stay, because it's useful information). As young women mature, a.k.a. hit puberty, they begin to menstruate—this is something we all know. But have you ever thought about how your period cycle might equate to the stars? It has more to do with astrology than you might think.

Let's talk about the Moon.

We have already talked about the Moon in-depth, including how it controls the tides and holds your emotions in your chart. But the Moon has even more power over us, due to both the close proximity to Earth and the limited time that the Moon spends within each sign. Beyond that, the Moon also has about a monthly cycle as it goes from New Moon to Waxing Moon, Full Moon, and Waning Moon. The moon phases move us across time, but also through the phases of your menstrual cycle. Mind. Blown.

Okay, maybe your mind is not that blown. Think about it like this: the Moon's cycle strongly correlates to your menstrual cycle, and the same amount of time elapses for each. Got it? Good.

There are a couple of phases of the Moon that are particularly important to note for your menstrual cycle: full moon and new moon. These two phases are not only important astrologically, but also about where you are in your cycle. Here is how the full and new moon impact your period:

New Moon: It is often said by some astrologers that the new moon is the part of your cycle where you are most fertile. <u>As an example source</u>, these astrologers say that the Moon and the menstrual cycle are related intermittently. Others say that the full moon is the highest fertility time, but some say it's not related at all. Now, this does not particularly matter to you, since you are probably not trying to have kids at the moment. However, it is imperative to note that when you are at this part of your cycle, the Moon is working in your favor. The new moon represents change, transformation, and entering a new cycle of your life. When we enter a new moon, we start new projects and accept transformation into our lives. The new moon is a time to set goals and intentions for yourself. You may feel cramps, have discharge, and feel that your body is preparing itself to move forward into your actual period. If this happens, you will start your period closer to the waxing moon, and not be fertile during the new moon. However, if you are not at this point in your cycle, you may experience this closer to the full moon, starting around then.

Full Moon: When we enter a full moon stage, we are finishing up our cycle. This means it is time to menstruate! As your uterine wall is shedding and you are bleeding, you are letting go of what no longer serves you. When a full moon is happening, we begin to see the achievement of our goals and move forward into new transformations. We are releasing anything negative so we may start a new journey. Thus, when we are on our period, we are shedding the bad vibes and inviting in the good ones. While your menstrual cycle may not always sync up completely with the Moon cycle, as it hasn't been fully shown to do so, it's still representative of an important part of a woman's life.

Now, the other phases of the Moon cycle are less relevant to your menstruation cycle. This is because as the Moon is waning and waxing, you are not having symptoms of fertility or menstruation. That doesn't mean that the Moon is not working with you! While not completely proven, the Moon is cycling alongside you through each phase of your menstrual cycle. Those cycles include menstrual phase, follicular phase, ovulation phase, and luteal phase.

So what does this have to do with Astrology?

Glad you asked. As you know by now, the Moon moves through each Zodiac sign every one to two days. That means that the full moon and new moon take place during a different Zodiac sign every month. You also know that each Zodiac sign has its own element that corresponds with it and different characteristics that accompany it, too. Thus, whatever Zodiac sign the Moon is in when it is full or new will influence our emotions and, consequently, our menstrual cycles.

Your cycle may not line up with the phases of the moon. This may happen because of a myriad of different reasons, but it is a completely normal and healthy occurrence.

Let's break it down really quick per Zodiac sign, shall we?

Aries: An Aries new moon will invite major changes into your life. This is a great time to think about your goals and aspirations, write them down, and invite positive change into your life. Likewise, when the full moon enters Aries, there will be a similar energy of change. You may feel more passionate and see your goals coming to life. Following your menstrual cycle, you will shed layers of who you are to become passionate about who you are becoming.

Taurus: A Taurus new moon invites you to be cozy, curled up with a blanket, and watching movies. While a Taurus full moon will have you feeling all kinds of stubbornness, there is a softness in the air that will invite you to spend some time alone and gather your thoughts. During these phases of your menstrual cycle, you will feel yourself being a little on edge, and it's imperative to remember to play nice with others.

Gemini: During a Gemini new and full moon, you will feel the need to ask questions and get answers. Gemini is all about learning and adapting to new situations. For your period cycle, you will find that you are open to new ways of life and feeling the release of the old all at the same time.

Cancer: You know by now that the Moon is at home in Cancer. Thus, a Cancer new moon will have you feeling

41

inspired and fulfilled. Likewise, a Cancer full moon will encourage you to do the things that make you feel happiest. For your menstrual cycle, you may feel more cramps than normal and need to give yourself time to rest and recoup.

Leo: During a Leo new moon you will feel refreshed and rejuvenated. Similarly, a Leo full moon will spring confidence on you in ways you have never felt before. Embrace that energy and allow your cycle to rid your body of toxic energy, inviting in that Leo sunshine.

Virgo: A Virgo new moon is all about tidying up. Clean your house; clean your life. Prepare your mind and body for all the new things you want in your life. Then when you see a Virgo full moon, you know how to cleanse your energy and prepare for a more organized future. Per your menstruation cycle, a Virgo moon of any kind may have you feeling a little overworked or exhausted, so make sure to make time for yourself to heal.

Libra: A Libra new moon is full of blessings and invites you to spoil yourself. Self-care is the name of the Libra game, and the full moon is no exception. Take some time for yourself, and whatever self-care looks like in your world, do it. The same goes for your menstrual cycle; take care of yourself and show yourself some love during a Libra moon of any kind.

Scorpio: A Scorpio new moon is full of mystery, and it's a great time to feel deeply and be introspective. A Scorpio full moon, however, will be a time of transformation for you. Per your cycle, you may feel that things are a little lighter during a

Scorpio moon, and take some time to be grateful for the blessings in your life.

Sagittarius: The fiery energy that comes with Sagittarius is ever-present in a new and full moon. Under Sagittarius, a new moon will spark impulsivity and a desire to try new things. A full moon will remind you to allow yourself to achieve your biggest dreams because they are within reach. Your cramps may be more intense and your flow heavier during a Sagittarius full moon.

Capricorn: During any kind of Capricorn moon, you will feel the urge to get to work. You may have a huge assignment due during this time or need to push through some other homework you have been avoiding. Utilize your time wisely during these moons! Your cycle may be delayed a little during a Capricorn moon due to stress or overwork. Make sure to take some time for yourself!

Aquarius: An Aquarius new moon is a great time to think about your life as it currently stands. Are you happy with the way things are going? What do you want to change? A full moon in Aquarius is when you can be your authentic self and embrace what makes you unique. Your cycle should be fairly normal (whatever normal looks like for you) during an Aquarius moon; no pressure either way.

Pisces: You may find yourself becoming super creative during a Pisces new moon. Delve into that creativity and use it to make new things for yourself. A Pisces full moon will reveal to you something you've always wanted to know. Your flow may be heavier during a Pisces moon, so be prepared for that, as you have an abundance of new ideas flowing through you, too.

Your cycle may not line up with the phases of the moon, and that's okay. A lot of what you have just read may contradict that. However, you know that your body is different from everyone else's in the world. No two people menstruate the same. So, you may not be totally in sync with the full moon, but that is nothing to worry about. The energies of each moon still align with your cycle. When you are bleeding, your body is in the full moon phase, and so forth and so on. Do not feel like something is wrong with you physically or astrologically if you do not line up precisely with the phases of the moon cycle.

As you also know, each Zodiac sign acts a little different, especially when on their period. There are always some things to look out for while menstruating to bring you back down to earth! Here is a quick rundown of how you may act, based on your sun sign, when on your period:

Aries: As an Aries, you are dynamic and passionate. You will try to re-channel the pain you feel during your period into different projects and activities.

Taurus: As a Taurus, you are sensual and have great strength. Because of this, when you are on your period you will use this time to recharge and reconnect with your body.

Gemini: Gemini, you are so curious and full of wonder. During your period, you will find yourself snacking quite a bit and learning new things, probably from YouTube videos.

Cancer: Cancer, you are always in touch with your emotions, and when you are on your period, that will only heighten. Thus, you may find yourself watching rom-coms and crying the night away (in a good way).

Leo: As a Leo, you are prideful yet dramatic. While you are on your period, you may find yourself bragging that you are on your period. Anyone else who is not menstruating better get out of the way!

Virgo: As a Virgo, you are very logical and love to feel like you're in control. When you're on your period, you have to release that control, which may be a little difficult for you. Deep breaths—it will be okay!

Libra: Libra, when you are on your period, self-care is the vibe. Make sure to pamper yourself and take care of your body!

Scorpio: If you are a Scorpio, you won't let your period slow you down. You will channel that energy into projects and activities that make you feel fulfilled.

Sagittarius: You love to laugh, Sagittarius, so you may find that when you are on your period you tend to crack jokes about it. Blame it on your period and have a good time regardless.

Capricorn: You are hardworking and determined, Capricorn, so you will try to ignore your period as much as possible. Nothing can stop you! It's okay to complain and let it out when you need to, though.

Aquarius: As an Aquarius, you love to be alone to process your thoughts and feelings. When you are on your period, you'll find that you're in for some much-needed "me" time. Embrace it!

Pisces: Pisces are innately emotional and creative, so when you are on your period, your emotions are heightened. You will channel this into some at-home projects and get back to feeling 100% in no time at all.

Well, there you have it! You should have a better understanding now of how the Moon and your sun sign interact with your menstrual cycle, and what to do going forward when the cramps get tough. You've got this!

Astrology & Your Parents

It probably comes as no surprise to you that you often find yourself fighting with your parents or not completely seeing eye to eye on some things. While that is completely normal in a teenager-parent relationship, it also has a lot to do with astrology too. Particularly focusing on your Moon and Venus signs, you can look at how you love, want to be loved, and how you carry those emotions. Likewise, you can check out your parents' charts too, and see what differs from (or is the same as) yours. You can do this with anyone's natal chart, of course, but when you look at the influence of the stars on your parents, it can be informative as to why they parent you the way that they do.

We are products of the environments that we are raised in. When you look at the astrological component of your chart versus your parents' charts, you can begin to unpack everything that you have gone through to get to where you are now. However, the most important signs to look at are the Moon, Venus, and Mercury signs. As a quick reminder:

The Moon rules emotions.
Venus rules love.
Mercury rules communication.

That being said, when you look at your parents' charts, you will want to see how they love, how they emotionally react, how they want to be loved, and how they think and communicate. At the end of the day, your parents are people, just like you. They have their own set of emotions and values that make up their special kind of magic. When you work to understand how their charts work, you can understand how you can work with them to create a cohesive, happy relationship between you.

Let's look at some solid examples, shall we?

Starting with the Moon…
We talk about the Moon a lot, and with good reason. Emotions are what fuel us, guide us, and thrive within us. Therefore, it makes sense that we might talk about the good ole' Moon a little too much. Regardless, when it comes to parenting, the Moon sign is key to understanding how your parents operate. Plus, it makes things a little easier on you, too.

Let's say that you have a Pisces moon, while your parent has an Aquarius moon.

There are a lot of pros and cons to this pairing. A Pisces moon is ever-emotional and creative and is often in a dreamy state of mind. Aquarius moons can relate to this, as they love to be alone and create their own special piece of the world. However, there may be friction here, because Aquarius moons will process their emotions internally, while Pisces moons process emotions externally. As a Pisces moon, you would feel everything very deeply. If you break up with someone, argue with a best friend, or even fail a math test, this could ruin your entire day. You could have a generally gloomy disposition when things don't go your way. When you get home from school, your Aquarius moon parent may not know exactly how to help you. This is because they don't relate to outwardly expressing emotion and may have trouble comforting others because of this. Thus, you may find yourself running off and feeling as though your parents don't care about your feelings.

This is not true. Well, in this made-up scenario, anyway. An Aquarius moon parent will be more reserved and want you to process emotions the way they do. So, when your Pisces moon wants to scream and cry from the rooftops, your parents may find themselves overwhelmed and unsure of how to handle it. The key, then, is to openly communicate and accept your parents for who they are. If you know that they process emotions internally, you won't take it personally when they try to understand why you're so upset. Likewise, if your parents understand that you are more emotionally loud than they are, they can learn techniques to be there for you in the way you need them to be. Thus, that's why learning your parents' moon signs are so important.

If you refer back to our *Big Three* section, you can see how each moon sign works within a chart. However, we are going to break down how each moon sign works *within the realm of parenting* to give you a better understanding of why your parents are the way they are. This way, you can take this information and use it to help you through those sticky situations with your parents and come out stronger on the other side.

Let's jump right into it. Here's a roundup of every moon sign and how it may impact parenting styles:

Aries moon parent: A parent with an Aries moon is going to be extremely passionate about their children. You'll find parents with this moon sign to be encouraging of every interest their kids have, almost to a fault. They want you to strive to be the best, and because of that, they can get frustrated easily when things don't go their (or your) way. They have good intentions at heart, so try to remember that whenever they get a little pushy.

Taurus moon parent: A Taurus moon parent is going to be very open-minded to whatever their kids want in life. However, the stubbornness that follows Taurus will creep up now and then. Taureans fear change and like things to be done their way. So, when a Taurus moon parent sets ground rules, they mean it, but they also want you to be inspired and follow your dreams. Cut them some slack when you can. They truly want to encourage you to be exactly who you are, but sometimes they just need some reassurance.

Gemini moon parent: A Gemini moon parent is going to be inquisitive. They love to ask questions and continue to learn about those they love. That being said, a Gemini moon parent will probably bug you a lot with questions, wanting to know everything about your life. They do this first and foremost because they care, but also so they can better understand how you operate in your life. The more you open up to their questions, the less they will ask!

Cancer moon parent: If you have a Cancer moon parent, chances are that they are very emotional. The proudest parents, Cancer moon parents will be at every sporting event and have the cameras waiting for every school dance photo op. Cancer moons also tend to snap at people with no warning, but it comes from the raw emotions they feel. Establish your boundaries with a Cancer moon parent, and they will respect them, keeping themselves in check while also being supportive of you!

Leo moon parent: Leos are the confident rulers of the Zodiac, for sure, and they are very prideful parents. They want the best for you and want to boost your success any way they can. A Leo moon parent will push you to be the best you can be and boast about you to anyone that will listen. When you find yourself resentful of this pridefulness, remember it comes from a place of utmost support and love for you in whatever you want to do. Leos are lions; they are pack animals that always put family first, and they truly want you to be successful in life.

Virgo moon parent: A Virgo moon parent wants to keep everything together as best they can. Virgo moons take on projects like they drink water, and because of that, they will be extremely busy. Virgo moon parents probably have a calendar on the fridge that is color-coded with everyone's schedules, and they like to keep the house in pristine condition. While this can get frustrating at times, it's important to be grateful for all that a Virgo moon does for their family, because things might just fall apart without them.

Libra moon parent: Libras love to keep things balanced; as a Libra moon parent, they will probably be the peacemakers of your family. Whenever you are hurting or something is wrong, Libra moon parents will provide you with extreme amounts of comfort. While they do often feel unsettled when things change, Libra moon parents have a calming energy that can help you through just about anything. They are indecisive, though, so when they can't make up their minds, sometimes they just need to be told what to do!

Scorpio moon parent: If your parent has a Scorpio moon, they are probably very internal. That means that they operate inside of their minds rather than talking through things outwardly. A Scorpio moon parent will try to shield their children from any trauma, taking it on themselves instead. They are protective of the ones they love and can be a little overprotective at times. That's okay, as long as you remind yourself that it's coming from a place of true love, rather than possessiveness.

Sagittarius moon parent: A parent with a Sagittarius moon is going to be a much more carefree kind of parent. They do not believe in micromanaging you, and instead want to give you the freedom to be completely yourself. Sagittarius people are adventurous and impulsive, always on to the next thing. As a result, a Sag moon parent will leave their kids alone for the most part and allow them the space to find their adventure. This can be frustrating as they are not always the most reliable, but know that there is still love there, always.

Capricorn moon parent: A Capricorn moon parent puts their value in hard work ethic. As long as you are trying hard at school, they won't be too hard on you. However, if you present a Capricorn moon parent with any kind of laziness, they will lose their patience with you rather quickly. If you are not a super organized hard worker, you may find conflict with your parents over it. However, if you show them that your way is still a way to get things done (with proof), they will see your efforts and know you still have goals to be reached.

Aquarius moon parent: Now, Aquarians are known for not always being the most emotional. They process things internally before they talk it through with others. That being said, if your parents have an Aquarius moon, they probably come off a bit standoffish and may be difficult to emotionally connect to. However, this does not diminish their love for you, and as long as you are openly communicating with them, they will always try their hardest to understand what you're going through.

Pisces moon parent: A Pisces moon parent is going to be extremely intuitive. This means that they are the ones likely to catch you sneaking out at 2:00 a.m., and they know right away when something is wrong. Pisces moons are in tune with their emotions and feel very deeply. When you argue, a Pisces moon parent will let everything out and are more receptive to open conversations. Especially as a parent, a Pisces moon will want to do everything they can to help, because they feel what you feel.

You know by now how important moon signs are; they hold space for your emotions and how you feel them. Likewise, when it comes to parenting, there is always a lot of emotion behind every parenting decision. Thus, your parents' moon signs play a huge role in how they interact with you, what rules they set, and generally how they are day to day. It is important to remember that in most cases, the way your parents emotionally react does truly come from a place of love.

Speaking of love, let's talk about Venus signs...

We have already gone through what Venus means in your chart. The planet Venus is the planet of love, ruling over Libra and Taurus. We don't talk about Venus a ton, but the planet is extremely significant when it comes to dating and parenting. Anything that involves *how* you love you can pretty much tie to Venus. Thus, when we talk about parenting, every parent will show their love in different ways. Venus highlights your love language, and it's important to know what your parents' love language is to understand how they treat you but also how they would like to be treated.

For example, let's say that your parents have a Taurus Venus. While Taurus is at home in Venus, it can cause some dissonance when it comes to parenting. Taurus people are big spenders and love to spoil those they love. They will cook great food, always making sure their loved ones are taken care of. This is a wonderful trait in Taurus; to be fiercely loyal and loving. However, a Taurus Venus is also stubborn and protective. While they love to spoil and give gifts, they need to receive validation from their loved ones. A Taurus is not one for change and wants everything to stay the same.

For a Taurus Venus parent, you may find that they can be stubborn with you and are the kind of parents that appreciate pleases and thank yous. Let them know you love them and appreciate all they do for you and stay calm when they get a little grumpy—that kind of thing.

So, now that you understand how a Venus placement works in the ways of parenting, let's get into the rundown of each Venus sign and how they impact parenting styles.

Aries Venus parent: An Aries Venus parent is extremely passionate and often non-committal and frustrated easily. You'll find that these parents are not the PTA type; rather, they show their love for their children by encouraging them to follow their passions. That said, an Aries Venus parent just wants to be appreciated, and they love surprises and thoughtful gestures. You will find conflict with an Aries Venus parent when they are disappointed, which can come off as frustration. However, it is because they love passionately and want the best for you.

Taurus Venus parent: We already went through what it's like to have a Taurus Venus parent, but to reiterate, a Taurus Venus parent is extremely grounded. They love to spoil their kids and give them pretty much anything they ask for. However, they can be stubborn and often won't budge when something goes against their values or plans. The key with a Taurus Venus parent is open communication and showing them through your words that you do value them in all areas of your life.

Gemini Venus parent: If your parents have a Gemini Venus placement, they will deeply value your words. A Gemini Venus parent is always learning and adapting to changes, so as you grow, they want to grow with you. They become frustrated when you shut them out, which can cause future conflict. To combat this, genuinely talking to them is the key. As long as they know where your head is at, a Gemini Venus parent will do what they can to support you in a way that fits both of your needs.

Cancer Venus parent: Parents with Cancer Venus placements are going to be emotionally charged when it comes to love. Any kind of thoughtful act of kindness will go a long way with a Cancer Venus; they love to be loved and cared for. During times of tension, a Cancer Venus may retreat because conflict frightens them. The solution is to be patient, and remember that your parents are people with feelings, too. Hugs go a long way!

Leo Venus parent: A Leo Venus parent will show their love through their pride. They are so proud of you, and no matter what you do in life (even if you make some bad decisions), they will always be proud of you. A Leo Venus parent will push you to be *the* best and will do everything in their power to support you. However, sometimes this behavior can feel suffocating, so it's important to set boundaries with your parents. Let them know when something is working, versus when it isn't.

Virgo Venus parent: A Virgo Venus parent is often extremely put together when it comes to love. They know exactly what they want and have high expectations for their loved ones. Sometimes a Virgo Venus can come on strong, as they hold their loved ones to a higher standard. Virgo Venus parents just want to be noticed for their efforts, and words of affirmation go a long way. When issues arise, make sure to communicate where you feel things went wrong; sometimes a Virgo Venus needs help seeing things from another perspective.

Libra Venus parent: Libra is at home in Venus and, like Taurus, Libras are pretty big spenders. In contrast, a Libra Venus will spend a lot of money on luxurious things, like going out to eat, bigger homes, furniture, and clothes. If you have a Libra Venus parent, you will rarely want for anything because they pride themselves on being providers for their loved ones. Conflict arises when a Libra Venus parent is selfish; to avoid this, make sure you tell them when you need their attention, and let them know that they are loved for who they are. Libra Venus parents always appreciate a little gift, too.

Scorpio Venus parent: A Scorpio Venus parent will hold on pretty tight. They love with great intensity, and because of that, you may find they can be strict when it comes to ground rules. Remind yourself that this comes from a place of love, and they want to make sure that you are always safe. A Scorpio Venus just needs confirmation that you are okay, and once you give that to them, it puts them at ease. They love small acts of kindness from their loved ones, even if it's something really simple.

Sagittarius Venus parent: A Sagittarius Venus parent will always push you out of your comfort zone- in a good way. They want their kids to be multifaceted and to always have fun in everything they do. That said, a Sagittarius Venus shows their love through having fun, and they love when their kids are up for adventures (think vacations and concerts). Sometimes Sagittarius Venus people can be impulsive, but they will always have your best interest at heart.

Capricorn Venus parent: A Capricorn Venus parent will have a hard outer shell but be a big softie on the inside. They show their love through hard work, which means that they are the surprise party planners and vacation guides, and they are always helping you get your homework done. Capricorn placements value hard work, but they also appreciate getting gifts and seeing others go out of their way to do something nice.

Aquarius Venus parent: Aquarius Venus people struggle within this placement because they are not always the most vocal with how they feel. Aquarius Venus parents value quality time above all else; they want to spend time with their kids and appreciate family movie nights and dinners. Conflict arises when they have a hard time expressing their love, but if they are inviting you to do something with them, just know that's how they show it. Expressing your interest in participating in things together is the best way to resolve any tension with an Aqua Venus.

Pisces Venus parent: Pisces Venus humans love to love and be loved. Almost to a fault, a Pisces Venus will go above and beyond for their children, always surprising them with gifts, hugs, and love. If you find yourself in a fight with a Pisces Venus, they will take everything very personally. They appreciate being loved and would rather talk through things than get into arguments. Because of this, a Pisces Venus parent will want to communicate with you when something is wrong, and they will do whatever they can to fix it.

We've talked a lot about emotions and love now with the Moon and Venus placements. Venus and the Moon are pivotal to understanding how your parents operate, how to approach them when there's tension between you, and how they need to be loved back (plus how *you* need to be loved, too!). Although, one of the most important elements in ANY relationship is…communication. It's true!

Most, if not all, families struggle with communication. You're around people that you are forced to like, even when they are not always the most likable. Family can be really difficult to navigate, but there is a level of trust and love there that is also hard to break. That being said, openly communicating with one another is going to be so important to keep your relationships joyous, cohesive, and going strong.

Mercury has entered the chat.

Mercury, as you now know, is the planet of communication. The planet that our Mercury is in tells us a lot about how we communicate with ourselves, and with others, too. Families, in general, are not always the perfect candidates for communication. However, the key to understanding your parents—and hopefully decreasing any arguments that may arise—is to understand how you both communicate. Think about it like this: every human being is different, and they each need to communicate in different ways. The way you communicate isn't always the way you need to be communicated to, and your Mercury sign can give you all the details on both.

One very important thing to note: When Mercury goes retrograde (which we have covered in previous sections), this means that everything is working backward. As a result, communication is completely thrown off. A Mercury retrograde will have you struggling to understand what others mean and miscommunicating what you mean throughout the entire period. Be aware of this, especially when it comes to your parents, so you can dodge any potential bullets.

If you take one thing away from this section, it should be the comparison of your Mercury sign with those of your parents. Never fear, we are going to break down each Mercury sign, and what that looks like in the realm of parenting, just for you.

Here are your parents' Mercury signs:

Aries Mercury parent: An Aries Mercury is quick to make decisions. They aren't impulsive, but they are rather impatient. If your parents have an Aries Mercury, they probably don't have time for indecision and will oftentimes make choices on your behalf. Aries Mercuries require instant gratification, and they can often miscommunicate what they mean, because they are onto the next thing. As long as you go along with them, they won't be frustrated; however, when their decision impacts you negatively, don't be afraid to calmly ask them for what it is you need.

Taurus Mercury parent: Taurus Mercuries are the epitome of "slow and steady wins the race." If your parents have a Taurus Mercury, they probably take their time with every decision they make. This may come across as laziness, but they're just thorough, and once they come to a decision, they will be stubborn about sticking to it. A Taurus Mercury is a great listener, as they think through each word before they speak it. When they take in new information, a Taurus Mercury wants to have all the evidence so they can help or make a choice. So, when you have news to share, make sure you can back it up!

Gemini Mercury parent: When your parents have a Gemini Mercury, they can come across as a little bit scatterbrained. This is because Gemini Mercuries have an interest in just about everything, and they seem to know a lot about every topic out there. Thus, they are thinking about a million things at once; when you talk to them, it can take them a few tries to download what you're saying, just as it takes them a while to convey what they mean to say. While this can be frustrating, remember that a Gemini Mercury just needs a bit of patience, but they always mean well.

Cancer Mercury parent: A Cancer Mercury person often acts strictly out of raw emotion. Because of this, you may find that they close up when it comes to conflict, and it can take a while before they respond. Cancers love to meditate and reflect on things before they come to a decision, and because of this, Cancer Mercury parents may need some time when arguments do arise. A Cancer Mercury parent will want to make sure they have the correct answer before they speak it and may require some patience from you before they get there.

Leo Mercury parent: Leo Mercuries will speak their minds, and they say everything with forceful pride. Often, Leo Mercury parents will come off as people who know it all, even when they don't; they want everyone in the room to know that they know everything. As a child of a Leo Mercury, it can sometimes feel isolating when you're wrong. However, a Leo Mercury parent just wants the best for their kids, so when they are coming off too prideful, just remember that it's coming from a place of love for you and not trying to discredit you.

Virgo Mercury parent: A Virgo Mercury parent will pay attention to the details. They are hardly ever boastful, and instead, they love when people acknowledge their smarts. When things are not in proper order, a Virgo Mercury can become a little high-strung. Thus, you'll find that they keep a neat and orderly home and can be a little hard on their children when things don't stay in top shape. However, what makes Virgo Mercuries great parents is their attention to detail; if you communicate your needs with them, they will remember what works best.

Libra Mercury parent: Libra Mercury people are very well received as far as communication goes. They believe in diplomacy and are always well mannered; Libra Mercuries rarely get into arguments, because they believe in keeping the peace. However, a Libra Mercury parent will be pretty indecisive when it comes to their kids (and most things, really). So, when approaching conflict, they won't always come to a quick decision, because they want to be diplomatic. While Libra Mercury parents are perfectionists, they often seek a compromise; when you bring them a problem, they will help you find the best solution for you by walking through different options objectively.

Scorpio Mercury parent: Scorpio Mercury parents want to get to the bottom of it. In almost every conversation, they dig to the depths of *why* you feel the way you do, *what* caused it, etc. These problem-solvers dig so deep that it can be a little overwhelming. However, a Scorpio Mercury is passionate about giving you advice that will help you, and they find value in open communication. That being said, cut them some slack, and know that their inquisitive nature is coming from a good place. They are masters at detecting secrets, so it's better to not keep much from them, too.

Sagittarius Mercury parent: Dreaming big is the name of the Sagittarius Mercury parent's game. While they often will have some holes in their arguments, Sag Mercury parents believe in freedom, especially when it comes to the thought process. They have big ideas and want to share them constantly with those they love. A Sagittarius Mercury parent may find it hard to come back down to Earth when reality sinks in, but that's okay; as long as you accept them for who they are, they will do the same for you.

Capricorn Mercury parent: A Capricorn Mercury parent will want to take their time to digest their food, metaphorically speaking. This means that when they are presented with new information, they need a little while to compartmentalize all of it. When you find yourself trying to communicate with your Capricorn Mercury parent, it could be frustrating for you because of their slower pace. Just know that they want to make sure they have all the facts straight before they get into it because they have your best interest at heart. They make decisions in a practical and personal way.

Aquarius Mercury parent: If you have an Aqua Mercury parent, you know that they love to break the rules. Aquarians in nature are independent thinkers that have unique ways of expressing themselves. So, when your parents have an Aquarius Mercury, you can expect them to handle every situation in a way that is unique to them. Aquarius people think logically in a way that only makes sense to them. Once you learn that, you can find out how you fit into their puzzle. Just remember to have an open mind! It's important to note that out of all the Mercury signs, Aqua Mercuries takes the most time to understand their point of view.

Pisces Mercury parent: Pisces Mercury people are extremely empathetic. They handle everything very gently because they can feel the raw emotions of everyone in the room. If you have a Pisces Mercury parent, you know that they react with deep emotion when you talk with them, as they outpour love and take on what you are feeling. Be patient with Pisces Mercuries, and trust that they are great listeners and want to help you in any way that they can. Pisces Mercury parents are known to tell white lies, but remember that it is because they simply want the ones they love to be comfortable and try not to fault them for it.

If you have taken anything away from this section on parenting, it should be this:

Most of the time, your parents are coming from a place of love. Accepting them where they are at is so important.

Communication is key. Remember to take what you now know about your parent's chart, compare it to yours, and find a communication style that works for you.

Once you do these two things, you can begin to mend some fences that may need to be fixed between you and your parents. They are people, too! With that also comes astrology. Everyone communicates differently, and sometimes it can be frustrating to deal with family members with a communication style you don't understand. You are not able to choose your family (like you would your friends...more on that in a few). However, that doesn't mean that you won't ever get along with your parents. They (most of the time) have your best interest at heart; they want to provide for you, help you, and watch you grow. Conflict is natural, but it's what you do with that conflict that makes the bigger impact. We would know.

P.S. To anyone who is struggling with their parents in a way that may be outside the zone of simply arguing and conflict, know that you are not alone. You can take the information here and try to solve these issues, but if you feel you are being abused or harmed in some way, please contact the police or someone you trust. Issues with parents are *normal*, and astrology does play a role in it. But remember that you know when something isn't normal, and you deserve to be healthy and happy. Help is out there!

When Things Get Hard

Trigger warning: talk of suicide, depression, anxiety, and other mental health issues/disorders.

As a teenager, you are probably no stranger to conflict and intense emotional reactions to things in your life. Most of us have struggled with others in our lives or have had issues with our mental health. There are a lot of stigmas out there about mental health, and people aren't always understanding. We know. However, there is certainly a crossover between astrology and mental health in that the stars tell us how we react in every situation.

That being said, let's look at some data available about teenagers and mental health, shall we?

According to the <u>World Health Organization (WHO)</u>, the age of adolescence is 10 to 19 years old. Here are some statistics from WHO about teenagers and mental health:

One in six people is aged 10–19 years.

Mental health conditions account for 16% of the global burden of disease and injury in people aged 10–19 years.

Half of all mental health conditions start at 14 years of age, but most cases are undetected and untreated.

Globally, depression is one of the leading causes of illness and disability among adolescents.

Suicide is the third leading cause of death in 15- to 19-year-olds.

The consequences of not addressing adolescent mental health conditions extend to adulthood impairing both physical and mental health and limiting opportunities to lead fulfilling lives as adults.

The concept of mental health covers a wide range of things, and it is different for every individual. ***Astrologers are not doctors, so if you need help, please seek it from professionals.*** However, astrology can look at the periods of your life and how you respond to different situations that involve your mental health. Some signs are more prone to anxiety than others, for example.

Beyond mental health, adolescence is no easy journey, it's true. You are going through puberty, and you will be feeling things at an insane level. There could be breakups, fights with your friends or family, embarrassment, excitement, and more. It's a whirlwind, and astrology can help you map it out just a little bit better.

In this section, we will break down mental health and teenage emotions per your planet placements. This gives a broad definition of how, say, Pisces placements (anyone that has Pisces in any of their planets) handle things in the face of adversity, or if Aries placements are prone to any mental health struggles. In reality, we all are, but astrology can help you understand your "why" and how to heal from there.

As a reminder: Your placements coincide with the planets and different aspects that they rule, so think about these guidelines in the terms of where they are placed in your chart. As an example, someone who has a Libra Mercury might feel anxiety about making decisions or being unfair to others, while someone with Mars in Pisces might feel guilty about being angry with others. It all depends on where things fall in your chart!

Are you ready? Let's jump right into it.

Mental Health and Your Sign

Our Zodiac sign tells us a lot about how we react to different situations, especially ones that are difficult on our mental health. In this section, we will break it down by the Zodiac sign, and you can apply it to where it falls in your chart. Each placement group will be broken down by how we respond to stressful situations, and what our overall mental health strength is, based on Zodiac signs.

Aries placements and mental health: We have talked about how Aries is one of the more passionate signs of the Zodiac. They give 110% to everything they do, often impulsively picking up new passions and diving right in. However, Aries does not often ask advice from others or look to their loved ones to confide in. Aries run from stressful situations, and because of this they often cause themselves new ones; this often results in migraines and physical body aches from exhaustion, as well.

What can help: Aries needs to find activities that are calming for them, that don't result in exhaustion.

Taurus placements and mental health: Taurus placements like to take their time and think practically about every given situation. When presented with something stressful, Taurus may find themselves staying home and running away from the conflict. While Taurus can be stubborn, they often want to take time to download the information at hand so they don't react harshly; however, if pushed before they are ready, Taurus can be rather angry and emotional. Taurus energy thrives on being subtle and grounded, but sometimes they can be pushed out of their comfort zone and can have a difficult time navigating those changes.

What can help: Taurus may find that cleaning or doing chores around the house help to empty their minds and relieve their stress. Likewise, a good movie and a soft blanket never hurts a Taurus, either.

Gemini placements and mental health: Gemini placements love to run away. When conflict or stress arises, Gemini will run as far as they possibly can. A Gemini will avoid stress and anxiety by throwing themselves into work and work-related things. Suppression is the name of the Gemini game, and they often will push themselves to the brink of exhaustion to avoid their feelings and emotions. How far is too far?

Geminis are not often known for being workaholics, but what makes them work so hard is their skill of avoidance.

What can help: Communication is always the key, especially for a Gemini. Talking it out with friends or grooving to some music can help release the stress and anxiety from Gemini placements.

Cancer placements and mental health: Cancer placements are extremely sensitive and emotional beings. That being said, they value alone time very deeply. Cancer does not want to trouble others with their problems and instead will retreat to their beds, getting cozy for hours at a time. Almost to a fault, Cancers will take as much time to themselves as they can, isolating from their loved ones and others around them. Cancer placements are prone to depression or intense anxiety, but they will often choose to deal with it on their own because they may feel like a burden to others.

What can help: Cancer placements want to retreat to things they like to do to help clear their minds. Finding something active to do that a Cancer likes will lift their happiness; getting them out of the house is the key.

Leo placements and mental health: Leo placements are not known for being emotional, but they very much are. When strife comes Leo's way, they will cry and talk it out, but not for long. Leos like to find the fun in every situation, and they will channel this into going out, socializing, and partying for sure. Thus, sometimes Leos won't take enough time to deal with what they are feeling, because they put on a facade of being completely fine. Leos are masters of distraction and will make sure that they are always having a good time, but this can be a problem when Leos don't make enough time in their schedules to cry and talk it out.

What can help: Leo placements need to talk through their problems, but don't like to be stuck at home. Going to dinner or out with a friend for a few hours can put a smile on a Leo's face.

Virgo placements and mental health: Virgos live in a land of worry. They like to create scenarios in their heads that are much worse than what is actually happening in front of them. Because of this, Virgos like to be left alone to deal with their problems. Virgos are critical of themselves and others to a fault, but especially themselves, which can cause an excess of stress and anxiety. When there's a conflict with others that causes Virgos stress, they will want to be completely alone to navigate how they want to react. If this boundary is not respected, Virgos can lash out and become very uncomfortable.

What can help: Virgos need time alone. Going for a walk, organizing their office supplies; any kind of solitude activity will help a Virgo come back to the center. Some alone time will do them good.

Libra placements and mental health: Libra placements value balance in all things. When that balance is thrown off, Libras will feel as if their world is crashing down around them. They are always looking for a solution to every problem to restore the peace that Libras crave. Libra placements don't often shut down, and instead, they are interested in getting advice and opinions from other people. Once they meet with their loved ones to discuss the issues at hand, Libras will listen intently and take that advice to heart, then work to restore the missing balance.

What can help: Libra placements need to find an activity that makes them feel balanced and at home; something peaceful that brings them back to the center.

Scorpio placements and mental health: Scorpio placements thrive on keeping everything a secret. Because of this, they often won't acknowledge that they are going through something. Often, Scorpios feel embarrassed when their mental health isn't great and will keep it to themselves until it is physically affecting their bodies. Scorpio placements have a hard time understanding that it is okay to go through these things and will be defensive if anyone reaches out and tries to help them. They often need space to figure things out for themselves, even if they want help from others or professionals.

What can help: Time. Scorpios need time to process what they are feeling and to come to a place where they feel okay enough to share with others or push through what's been happening with them.

Sagittarius placements and mental health: Sagittarius placements are a lot like Leos in that they surround themselves with others and try to run from their problems. Sag's love to make a joke about their problems and throw themselves into work or play instead of dealing with what's going on. Sagittarius people do not like to be left alone, constantly wanting to go out and be around other people to avoid their problems. As a result, things can get bottled up and eventually implode for a Sagittarius, unless they do the work to release it.

What can help: Any kind of adventure or travel can help to relieve a Sagittarius placement's stress and help them to live happier lives.

Capricorn placements and mental health: A Capricorn placement is a master of disguise. When they struggle with stress, Capricorns will find the most logical way to get out of the stressful situation. Because of this, it will almost always seem like a Capricorn has it all together. However, the reality is that Capricorns are hiding from their problems just like the rest of us. They convince themselves that everything is fine without dealing with the problems at hand. This technique can work for a while, but it can cause a Capricorn to fall apart all at once if not worked through properly.

What can help: Capricorn placements need a practical technique to work through things: Journaling, meditating, scheduling time every day to better themselves. You get the idea.

Aquarius placements and mental health: Aquarius placements live in the future rather than the present or the past. That said, Aquarius people will be in their heads almost all of the time and forget to take care of their mental health as a result. All that planning for the future can cause a new kind of stress, and often Aqua placements will miss it completely. Aquarius people detach themselves from their emotions and the emotions of others, which is never the healthiest way to live.

What can help: Aquarius placements need a reality check; something that can bring them back into the present. That can be as simple as reading a book, talking with a friend, or watching a movie—something that breaks them away from all that future planning they are doing.

Pisces placements and mental health: Pisces placements can be good at eliminating stress from their lives because they simply imagine that they are not stressed. Sounds easy enough, right? However, Pisces spend so much time caring about other people and their stress that sometimes they forget to take care of themselves. Pisces take on the emotions of others easily, and that can damage their emotional well-being. They spend ample time preaching about self-care, yet often forget to care for themselves in the process.

What can help: Pisces need a self-care routine. Finding small things that make them happy can go a long way for a Pisces; anything creative or comforting in some way.

No matter how old you are, your mental health matters. Self-care and knowing the foundation of who you are can go a long way. That's where astrology comes into play. Understanding yourself and those around you through the stars, planets, and universe can help you find ways to improve your life. Thus, astrology can help you a lot with tackling mental health issues and helping others around you as well.

In this next section, we will briefly break down the Zodiac placements once again, this time focusing on what each placement truly needs. You can use this guide to help out a friend who is struggling or look through your planet placements and see what you could be needing right now. Regardless of how you use it, here is how astrology can help each Zodiac placement with their mental health and care.

Get in there!

Aries placements and their needs: Aries placements are passionate and impulsive, which can make them impatient when their needs are not met. That said, when an Aries placement is struggling, it may be difficult to figure out how to help them. An Aries can lash out when they are having a hard time and make others around them feel small. Knowing that is the key because then you can rise above it. Don't take their anger personally, and redirect the conversation to find out what's bothering them.

What can help: Cook an Aries dinner, pick out their favorite movie or game, and let them simply be. They appreciate the little things, even if they don't often show it.

Taurus placements and their needs: Taurus placements are very slow to get going, and they can be stubborn along the way. Because of this, a Taurus placement may need space when they are struggling with something. However, Taurus placements love to be comforted, and so they can be difficult to navigate when they are going through something. Give

.

them time to figure it out while also lending your shoulder for them to cry on if needed.

What can help: Think all things comfort when it comes to helping Taurus placements. Blankets, cozy socks, tea, some good old comfort food. Taurus people just want to snuggle and feel loved!

Gemini placements and their needs: Gemini placements like to do things on their own. They are independent to a fault and often process things internally. However, Geminis love when the people in their lives are thoughtful. Often, Geminis are solving life's puzzles in their heads and don't think anyone is noticing what they are going through. If you take time out of your day to give a Gemini a little love, it will go a long way.

What can help: Small gifts that Geminis will like, a text asking if they are doing okay- little things like that are Gemini's bread and butter.

Cancer placements and their needs: As you know by now, Cancers are extremely sensitive beings. Not to beat a dead horse here, but Cancers do tend to feel things very deeply and as such, are prone to crying things out. If left to their own devices, a Cancer won't get out of bed for days and can have a lot of trouble getting back to a routine when they are struggling. Cancers require patience from their friends and family, and lots of love, too.

What can help: Cancers sometimes need a little motivation. Getting them out of bed and into the world again can help a lot, as well as holding their hands and comforting them, too.

Leo placements and their needs: Leos are inherently prideful, and they will present to their loved ones as if everything is fine. They want to shake it off, go out, and have a good time. This is all well and good, but they can become kind of toxic when they throw all their problems to the wind and decide to ignore them instead of addressing them. As a friend to a Leo, it can be confusing as to how to best approach them about this. Give them the space to find it on their own, while also giving them a little push to get there.

What can help: Let your Leo shine bright and go out and have a good time. When that's said and done, bring them back to center, and try to talk things out with them, too. A little balance never hurts anyone.

Virgo placements and their needs: Virgo placements can sometimes be hard to read. They are well organized, and throw themselves into cooking, cleaning, and other work when they are struggling. That said, it can be hard to crack their outer shells and dig deeper, because they are trying to repress all of that. While a level of distraction can be a great thing for their mental health, they also will need a push to address what is going on with them. Be patient and open, and your Virgo will eventually open up.

What can help: Let your Virgo friend know that you are here for them. Text them to see if they need anything and offer your support any way you can. They will come to you when they're ready!

Libra placements and their needs: Libra placements carry their mental health struggles well. They think so logically that they are some of the best problem solvers. They can take any given situation and solve it in their own Libra way. Because of this, Libras have a hard time expressing themselves when they are struggling; they genuinely believe that everything is fine, even when it isn't. Sometimes a Libra will need a nudge in the right direction so that they can delve into what is going on, without trying so hard to maintain the balance.

What can help: Sitting down to talk with your Libra friend will be the key here. Highlight to them some things you have noticed and offer constant reassurance their way. Talk logically to them, and they will pick up what you're putting down right away.

Scorpio placements and their needs: Scorpios will hold everything in until it finally bursts out of them all at once. As a result, they can be pretty harsh when people try to help them; Scorpios get defensive when they are hurting. Give a Scorpio placement space to figure things out on their own; sometimes they just need time away to deal with everything that is going on. However, always offer them a listening ear, and when the time feels right, they will talk through it.

What can help: Small gestures of kindness go a long way with a Scorpio. They often think that no one cares about them, and they will appreciate the little things.

Sagittarius placements and their needs: A Sagittarius placement is going to avoid their problems like the plague. They will want to go out and party it out, spending as much time around other people as possible. Sagittarians are not ones to wallow, and instead, they want to go-go-go. As a result, they push their problems deep inside and may have trouble communicating them to others. It can be difficult to talk through things with a Sagittarius, but it's important to bring them back down to earth sometimes and remind them that it's okay to be vulnerable.

What can help: Sagittarius placements want freedom and independence. Sometimes, joining in on their fun can help them move forward. Let them be, and they will oftentimes find their way back.

Capricorn placements and their needs: Similar to Sagittarius, Capricorns also like to bury things deep down and keep on truckin'. However, a Capricorn will avoid their problems by throwing themselves into their work, taking on new projects, and thinking about pretty much nothing but their career or what they are working on. Because of this, a Capricorn has no time to waste on anxiety and instead overcompensates by exhausting themselves at work. Communicating with a Capricorn placement can be difficult at times, but they mean well.

What can help: Helping a Capricorn placement come to a stopping point will help them to heal what's going on with them. They often need to be reminded to slow down and take things easy.

Aquarius placements and their needs: Every Aquarius is different from the next. Because they are so unique, it can be difficult to pin down what exactly they need from their friends and loved ones. Aqua placements are usually introverted, and they need to think things through on their own because they live in a future that no one else understands. This can be a little exhausting and may require patience from loved ones as they hear their Aquarian friends repeat the same topics over and over.

What can help: Bring your Aqua friend back into reality and help them to remember things going on in the present that they are grateful for. Help them remember the things they need to deal with—since they are in their heads a lot of the time, sometimes they need a little push to get stuff done.

Pisces placements and their needs: Pisces placements will find themselves caring for others above themselves almost always. Because of this, when it comes to their own needs, they often throw those aside. Pisces are prone to anxiety because they want to please everyone, which can tear them down. In doing so, Pisces retreat into their dream worlds and are masters at avoiding confrontation. Sometimes Pisces need a little push to get back to their happier selves and need to be reminded of the good things in their lives.

What can help: Pisces placements need to be reminded of the people they have in their lives that love them. Offering support and telling Pisces that you're there for them goes a long way, as they don't always realize they don't have to carry things alone.

Talking about mental health and your struggles is so important especially at younger ages. Astrology can help you figure out what you need and how you react when stress enters your life. While astrologers are not doctors, astrology can be utilized to help you discover parts of your personality you may not have otherwise known before. When you delve deep into your natal chart, you can pinpoint the things that cause you stress and anxiety and what helps to relieve it.

If you are struggling, here are some resources that can help:

National Suicide Prevention Hotline
Call 1-800-273-TALK (8255)

Crisis Text Line
Text "HELLO" to 741741

For more information, visit NIMH.nih.gov.

Astrology & Relationships

If you have made it this far, you know by now that astrology plays a role in pretty much every area of your life. That being said, why wouldn't it apply to your dating life, too?

You probably have seen how common it is to reference astrology when talking about dating. As a teenager, you probably are just beginning to dabble in dating. Or maybe you have been wanting to date but are nervous or haven't started yet. Some of you may have parents that frown upon dating so young, and that's okay! In this section, we will be talking about sign compatibility, what works with dating and what doesn't, your Venus sign, and more. If you can't apply this info to your life now, you can utilize it later once when you are ready to dive into the dating pool.

Relationships of any kind can be quite stressful. You are deciding every day to be a part of someone else's life and allow them to be part of yours. We've covered relationships regarding your parents, yourself, and your friends (about how to help them through various issues). However, dating relationships are another beast entirely. When feelings are involved, especially during adolescence, things are taken to a whole other level. That said, astrology can help you navigate those waters and learn a lot about you and your partners along the way.

Remember your good old Venus sign? She comes into play once again when it comes to dating and relationships, and we're going to break it down for you. Hang in there, we will get to sign compatibility too, don't you worry.

Venus Signs and Dating

Venus is the planet of love, which you know well by now. It rules over Taurus and Libra and loves all things beauty and love-related. With your parents and your friends, Venus tells you how they love you and what your love languages are. In other words, Venus tells you what you need from loved ones to feel your best in those relationships. When it comes to dating, however, Venus can tell you a lot more.

Your Venus sign in a relationship is in the driver's seat. It tells you which direction to go, when to slam on the breaks, and when it's full speed ahead. Depending on what sign your Venus is in, it can also dictate how you act in a relationship. Are you clingy or more of a free spirit? Do you date a lot of people at once or one at a time? You can find all of the answers in your Venus placements.

Don't fret, darling, we are going to break down each Venus placement once again. This time, though, we will look at how your Venus sign impacts your dating life. (It's also a great time to look at your partner's Venus sign, you know, while you're already here…)

Before we get down to the nitty-gritty of the Venus signs, it's also important to look at the major love languages, since each Venus sign has one. If you are not familiar with the love languages, they are:

Words of Affirmation
Quality Time
Physical Touch
Acts of Service
Receiving Gifts

We will delve into the love languages and which Venus sign has which love language. If you're interested in learning more about the love languages in-depth, you can head to Very Well Mind!

Let's jump right into it.

Aries Venus and dating: An Aries Venus is passionate in a relationship. Surprise, surprise! They love with intensity and are happy to jump straight into relationships. However, Aries is not a sign that particularly loves to be tied down. Thus, in a relationship, Aries Venus natives may find that they have a hard time being told what to do or how to act. When conflict arises, Aries Venuses will react out of anger and may find that they get defensive or snap at their partners easily. This anger comes from a place of passion, and the inner fire of Aries comes out in Venus. While Aries Venus people don't often settle, they can learn to channel their anger into something productive; because the anger of Aries comes from love, and they do want to date and be in love, too. Sometimes it just takes time and patience.

Aries Venus Love Language: Words of affirmation. Aries Venus people express their love through words, and also need words of affirmation back. Think "I love you's" before getting off the phone.

Taurus Venus and dating: A Taurus Venus will feel completely at home in a relationship. Taurus Venus natives love to love and be loved. Comfort is the name of the Taurus game, and you'll find that they love to cuddle and are almost always in relationships. However, Taurus Venus people do have a stubborn streak in them. When their partner calls them out about something or asks them to do something they don't want to do, a Taurus Venus may become defensive and begin acting impossible. Taurus is not a sign that does well with change, so when presenting new information, it's important to tread lightly and calmly. If your partner has a Taurus Venus, though, they do love to give gifts and cook when they are dating someone, and you'll find that they can be very gentle and sweet.

Taurus Venus Love Language: Physical touch. Taurus Venus natives love to cuddle and crave closeness. Think holding hands and snuggling while watching movies; that's the stuff a Taurus Venus loves.

Gemini Venus and dating: Gemini Venus natives are great listeners. They love to learn and will always help guide the conversation as you begin to date. However, Gemini Venus people can be hard cookies to crack. They are not always forthcoming about themselves, so it can feel a little uneven when they are learning so much about you. Gemini is a more private sign despite being very social, and because of that, it can take them a while to open up. Once they do, though, they won't be able to stop talking and telling you everything you've ever wanted to know. Deep conversations are what make Geminis so cool, and if you're into that kind of thing, a Gemini Venus is a great partner.

Gemini Venus Love Language: Quality time. It's no secret that deep conversations over a cup of warm coffee could be considered quality time together, and that's the kind of thing a Gemini thrives on.

Cancer Venus and dating: A Cancer Venus wants one thing and one thing only: to take care of the ones they love. Think of Cancer as simultaneously being the mom and baby of the Zodiac. They are extremely emotional and require a lot of care, but they also want to make sure you are well taken care of, too. Because of this, Cancers are appreciative of just about anything anyone does for them. They love to love, and they feel connected deeply to the ones they date. Cancer Venus will always be there for you and are loyal almost to a fault, but they value it greatly when their loyalty is returned to them from their partners. If your partner is Cancer Venus, you can rest assured that they only have eyes for you and are happy to be living life with you by their side.

Cancer Venus Love Language: Acts of service. Cancer Venus natives will appreciate any kind of thoughtful act. If you pick a flower from your garden for them or donate to their favorite charity…they notice the little things, and truly fall in love with the people who do them.

Leo Venus and dating: Leo Venus people already know that they rock. There's no question in their minds that they are pretty great partners. However, Leos are more emotional than we often give them credit for, and they can sometimes become insecure in relationships. Leo Venus natives need to know that their love is returned to them, or they have a tendency to dominate in the relationship otherwise. A Leo Venus wants to know that you are paying attention to them and not wasting their time, because they know that their time is valuable. If you aren't treating them right, they'll be the first to say it. On the flip side, if they aren't treating you right, they'll expect you to talk to them about it so that they can work to fix it.

Leo Venus Love Language: Words of affirmation. Leos may already know they are wonderful partners, but they need to know that you are listening to them. Sometimes even the most prideful of the pack can have issues with self-confidence, and that's okay; they just need a little reassurance sometimes.

Virgo Venus and dating: A Virgo Venus native will always be working hard and be passionate about the things they care about. That said, when it comes to relationships, Virgo Venus people can be hard to figure out. They are fiercely loyal and want to push their partners to do and be their absolute best. Virgo is the sign of service, and they believe that if they push themselves hard enough, they will do good things for the world. Thus, they hold their partners to the same high standards; they truly believe in their greatness. A Virgo Venus will keep whoever they are dating in line and help them to find their passions and achieve their dreams right alongside one another.

Virgo Venus Love Language: Acts of service. It should come as no surprise that Virgos value acts of service; they are working hard to support you and expect a level of support back. That said, when you do something nice for them, it may surprise them, and they will appreciate it exponentially.

Libra Venus and dating: A Libra Venus loves to live a life of luxury. While this sounds like maybe Libras spend a little too much money (which is true), it means that they love to fill their lives with things that make them happy. It's no surprise that Libras also seek out other people who make them happy and love to spoil them, too. Libras love to love, as the sign itself is ruled by Venus, and you will often find them bouncing from relationship to relationship. However, when a Libra finds "the one," they are locked in; they are very loyal to their partners and believe in the truest form of love. If you're looking for a serial monogamist, look no further than a Libra Venus.

Libra Venus Love Language: Gift Giving. Since Libra Venus natives love to spoil themselves with things that spark joy, they also love to do it for those they love. When a Libra Venus is smitten, expect that they will shower their partner in gifts, because that's how they show their love.

Scorpio Venus and dating: Affection is the name of the Scorpio Venus game. Scorpio Venus humans need constant validation from their loved ones and hold on extremely tight to those they are fond of. They can be a little possessive, and in that, they also have a knack for detail. A Scorpio Venus will catch on rather quickly to pretty much anything; their keen eye will notice right away when something isn't right. They have a strong grip on those they love and can be protective of their partner's energy and love strongly, too.

Scorpio Venus Love Language: Physical touch. A Scorpio Venus loves to be affectionate and will show it through touching their partner frequently. While they may not like to touch other people, in a relationship, a Scorpio Venus will want to hold hands pretty much 24/7.

Sagittarius Venus and dating: A Sagittarius Venus, as you have probably guessed, is the life of the party. They love to go on adventures, especially when they are in a relationship. As a result, a Sagittarius Venus native will often take dating to the next level by taking their partner (or partners) on simply amazing dates. From hiking to concerts to skydiving, expect a Sagittarius Venus to live a somewhat crazy life, but one that is full of fun. If you're looking for a good time, call up a Sag Venus.

Sagittarius Venus Love Language: Quality time. It should come as no surprise that a Sag Venus would be after quality time. They deeply value their partners and want to have the best time with them. A Sagittarius Venus shows their love by taking their loved ones on adventures, making quality time their MO.

Capricorn Venus and dating: Capricorn Venus natives have extreme amounts of ambition. They love to work and achieve the goals they set for themselves (true Cap nature). That said, a Capricorn Venus will expect their partners to have similar drives to them; they want someone who they can compete with, healthily. A Capricorn Venus will not ask for much, but they do like to know that you know they work hard. Everything about Capricorn energy screams determination and high standards, and a Capricorn Venus will bring that on the field of the game called dating.

Capricorn Venus Love Language: Gift giving. Funny enough, a Capricorn Venus native will love to give and receive gifts as well. They like to know that their hard work is appreciated, and they show their appreciation through giving from that hard work as well. They're just big softies beneath that outer shell.

Aquarius Venus and dating: While an Aquarius Venus may have a difficult time expressing their emotions outwardly (if they even have them, that is), they crave a world of inner and outer peace. Aqua Venus natives just want everyone to get along; they love when others go above and beyond to do something nice for someone. Everyone deserves happiness in the eyes of an Aquarius Venus, and in a relationship, they do their part to ensure that their partner feels validated and loved. An Aquarius Venus doesn't care about balance; rather, they just want everyone to be kind and understand that we are all simply human.

Aquarius Venus Love Language: Acts of service. If you go out of your way to do something nice for an Aqua Venus, this will show them that you care. They spend lots of time doing acts of service for others and feel very seen and loved when someone does one for them.

Pisces Venus and dating: A Pisces Venus native will value alone time more than just about anything. When they are in their dream-like states, a Pisces Venus needs some time to find their way back to reality. That said, a Pisces Venus will love spending time with their partner once they are out of their head. They love cozy date nights, and when they learn something new about their partner, they never forget it. Pisces Venus people love to spoil their loved ones, especially when they are dating someone (old or new). A Pisces Venus takes their time and slowly learns as much as they can about their partners, to spend time together doing things they both love to do.

Pisces Venus Love Language: Quality time. Everything about Venus in Pisces screams *time*. They take their time getting to know their partners and deeply value the time spent together. A Pisces Venus will prefer a movie night over gifts or adventures. They want to get to know you and spend some one-on-one time with you.

Whew, we did it! Now you should know what you and your partner's Venus signs are and the corresponding love languages with both. With that insight, you can remember what your partner's love language is and work toward doing things that make them (and you) happy. If you're not dating anyone, you can still take away what your love language is and spend some quality time with yourself. Self-care, baby!

Likewise, if you are currently single or looking to jump into dating, we are going to break down sign compatibility. You can even refer to this if you are in a relationship or just want to see how your sign interacts with others (friends, parents, or otherwise). While we will be focusing on dating compatibility for this section, it can't hurt to give it a look anyway.

How it works: We will be going by general placements/sun sign. Since your sun sign is the foundation of who you are, it generally says the most about your personality. Think of it as the framework of you; we will be taking your framework and comparing it to all the other sun signs in the Zodiac. Why? To show you how compatible you are with the other signs, or even your sign, of course! We will show you the sun sign you are most and least compatible with and give you the rundown of each sign and what does and doesn't work. Other placements in your chart will impact your compatibility, but this gives you a good starting point based on your sun sign.

If that still doesn't make sense, don't worry, you'll understand it once we start going. Are you in? Let's get the ball rolling, starting with Aries...

Zodiac Sun Sign Compatibility

Aries

Most compatible Zodiac sign: Gemini
Least compatible Zodiac sign: Capricorn

Compatibility Zodiac Sign Ranking for Aries:

Aries - Low
Taurus - Low
Gemini - High
Cancer - Medium
Leo - High
Virgo - Low
Libra - Low
Scorpio - High
Sagittarius - High
Capricorn - Low
Aquarius - High
Pisces - Medium

Aries is the first sign of the Zodiac year, and also the first fire sign. Aries people are ruled by passion and don't like to be tied down to any person, place, or thing. As a result, Aries is rather free-spirited and wants to have an adventure and new experiences. An Aries native does not do well with conflict and can get heated when arguments arise. They are confident and natural-born leaders, but often don't have time for tiny details, moving quickly into the next thing.

Gemini is the strongest match for Aries because they are learners, not leaders. Geminis love to take on new projects and learn new information, which an Aries is happy to give. This makes for a harmonious pairing. However, Aries does not mesh well with Capricorn. Capricorn humans pay way too much attention to detail and encourage structure in all areas of their lives. Aries is unhappy with Capricorn because Aries people do not like to feel settled; rather, they want to pay as little attention as possible to details and go about their way.

Aries people can throw tantrums now and then when things don't go their way. However, if you are looking for someone who loves adventure and is passionate about everything they do, an Aries partner may be for you. They are ambitious in their own right, and Aries people are optimistic in every sense of the word.

Taurus

Most compatible Zodiac sign: Taurus
Least compatible Zodiac sign: Aries

Compatibility Zodiac Sign Ranking for Taurus:

Aries - Low
Taurus - High
Gemini - Low
Cancer - High
Leo - Medium
Virgo - High
Libra - Medium
Scorpio - High
Sagittarius - Low
Capricorn - High
Aquarius - Low
Pisces - High

Taurus is the first earth sign of the Zodiac; earth signs are dependable and grounded. That said, a Taurus is known to be stubborn because they fear change. Romantically, a Taurus will be a caretaker; they love to cook and spoil their partners. However, Taurus humans are serial monogamists, basically meaning that they mate for life. You won't find a Taurus is open for much outside of their plans, but they go above and beyond for their loved ones.

It should come as no surprise, then, that Taurus natives often find themselves in relationships with other Taurus natives. No one loves a Taurus like a Taurus! Their earthy energy makes quite a pair, and they can appreciate the stubbornness in one another that evens out quite nicely. In contrast, Aries struggles with the stubborn aspects of Taurus. Aries craves change and are ever-evolving, while Taurus just wants things to stay the same. As a result, there is a lot of friction in an Aries-Taurus couple.

Taurus can be reluctant to change in the face of adversity. However, if you are looking for a partner that will love to cook, cuddle, and take care of you—Taurus energy is your perfect match. Taurus natives give 110% of themselves to their partners, and love to support them in any way that they can.

Gemini

Most compatible Zodiac sign: Aries
Least compatible Zodiac sign: Cancer

Compatibility Zodiac Sign Ranking for Gemini:

Aries - High
Taurus - Low
Gemini - Medium
Cancer - Low
Leo - High
Virgo - Medium
Libra - High
Scorpio - Low
Sagittarius - Medium
Capricorn - Medium
Aquarius - High
Pisces - Low

Gemini is the first air sign of the Zodiac! Air signs love to learn new things, especially those with Gemini in their charts. A Gemini wakes up each day and is a new person; for better or worse. That said, a Gemini partner makes for a good listener because they want to learn everything about those they love; they are receptive to new ideas. Geminis can be a little moody at times, and they sometimes have rain clouds above their heads for a few days. However, they value a partner who is down to spend time with them and listen as well as they do.

Since Geminis are naturally inquisitive, they are always down for a good time. A Gemini native will want to explore new things with their partners and don't mind changing things up. That said, the best match for a Gemini is Aries! Aries and Gemini's energy complement each other because they are both open to change and impulsivity. However, Cancer makes for a weaker pair with Gemini. This is because Cancers are extremely emotional and introspective;

Geminis (as an air sign) often don't care to have their emotions on display, especially in public. As a result, Cancer's emotional outbursts cause stress for Gemini placements, making them the least compatible.

Gemini's adaptability is a great asset in a relationship because they can pinpoint exactly what their partner needs. Geminis love to give in relationships but are open to receiving, as well, which creates a natural balance. While they can be a bit moody and on edge, Geminis can recover quickly if given the space to do so. Gemini natives are not the most outwardly emotional but are deeply understanding, which can help in relationships.

Cancer

Most compatible Zodiac sign: Taurus
Least compatible Zodiac sign: Capricorn

Compatibility Zodiac Sign Ranking for Cancer:

Aries - Medium
Taurus - High
Gemini - Low
Cancer - Medium
Leo - High
Virgo - Medium
Libra - Low
Scorpio - High
Sagittarius - Low
Capricorn - Low

Aquarius - Low

Pisces - High

Cancers are the first water sign of the Zodiac, and it is ruled directly by the Moon as are our emotions. Cancers are so in tune with their emotions that sometimes it is all-consuming; they can be master manipulators without even meaning to because their emotions are so strong. However, Cancers have a love for all things cozy, and they make great partners for those who enjoy taking care of one another.

Cancers love to be taken care of and thrive when their partners are extremely supportive of them. Thus, Taurus is the perfect pair for a Cancer person. Taurus and Cancer both love to be cozy; think movie nights on the couch. Taurus humans want to take care of their partners and take on a mothering role which is perfect for emotional Cancer energy. In contrast, Cancers do not pair well with Capricorn energy. Capricorns are fiercely independent and do not have time to dwell on things they deem unimportant. As a result, Capricorns are not often in touch with their emotions, and they would rather be working on new projects; this directly conflicts with the slow-paced, watery Cancer.

Cancer natives are great partners; they love to love and feel very deeply about those in their lives. While they are prone to emotional outbursts, Cancers do have good hearts and mean well in all that they do. If you're looking for someone who is in touch with your emotions, too, look no further than Cancer.

Leo

Most compatible Zodiac sign: Aries
Least compatible Zodiac sign: Capricorn
Compatibility Zodiac Sign Ranking for Leo:

Aries - High
Taurus - Medium
Gemini - High
Cancer - High
Leo - Low
Virgo - Low
Libra - High
Scorpio - Low
Sagittarius - High
Capricorn - Low
Aquarius - Low
Pisces - Medium

Leos are human forms of sunshine; they light up every room they walk into. In relationships, Leos help their partners to feel more confident by being their cheerleaders. While they are extremely positive, Leos are also in touch with their emotional sides as well. Sometimes, Leo's emotions can come out through tantrums but know that they always come from a place of care. Leos want the best for whoever they are around and work hard to make people feel loved.

This probably comes as no surprise, but Leo's best match is Aries. Why? Aries' and Leo's energy are very similar. They are both fire signs that crave positivity and adventure. Aries will push Leo out of their comfort zone, and Leo will work to make Aries feel much more confident in themselves. While they could be prone to arguing, they move on quickly and maintain a positive attitude. In contrast, Capricorn is the weakest pairing for Leo. Capricorns value structure and want everything to be the way *they* want it. A Leo challenges Capricorn's energy because Leos are creative and never want to settle in one place.

If you are looking to date someone that makes you feel like your best self, look no further than Leo natives. Leos want you to shine just as bright as they do, and they will do everything in their power to make that happen. While they can be a little defensive when they feel attacked and are quick to anger, they try their hardest to always be optimistic.

Virgo

Most compatible Zodiac sign: Scorpio
Least compatible Zodiac sign: Libra
Compatibility Zodiac Sign Ranking for Virgo:

Aries - Low
Taurus - High
Gemini - Medium
Cancer - Medium
Leo - Low
Virgo - Medium
Libra - Low
Scorpio - High
Sagittarius - Low
Capricorn - High
Aquarius - Low

Virgos are extremely detail-oriented people who are caring and value level-headedness. That said, a Virgo will always notice the little things about their partners. If you say you want something in passing, the next day a Virgo will have it for you. They are grounded, organized, and great problem solvers. While Virgos are pretty modest and reserved, they still like to have fun sometimes, too. They can be a little judgmental when provoked, but they often find partners that help to level them out.

Thus, the best partner for Virgo is Scorpio. Virgos need a partner that is curious, but level-headed. Scorpios think logically about most things, but they are very introspective. A Virgo will notice when Scorpio is gloomy and will help to bring their energy back up. Scorpios are attentive to detail in the same way as a Virgo, making them a perfect pair. In contrast, Virgos don't mesh as well with Libra energy because a Libra's is much louder. Libras love fashion, fun, and being the center of attention while Virgo likes to hide in the background. Because of this, Libras make Virgos uncomfortable and can cause a lot of friction due to Virgos wanting to stay in their comfort zone.

Virgos care much more than they may let on; their attentiveness is a plus when it comes to relationships. A Virgo native wants to be comfortable with whoever they are around and strive to make their partners feel the same way.

Libra

Most compatible Zodiac sign: Gemini
Least compatible Zodiac sign: Capricorn

Compatibility Zodiac Sign Ranking for Libra:

Aries - Low
Taurus - Medium
Gemini - High
Cancer - Low
Leo - High
Virgo - Low
Libra - High
Scorpio - Low
Sagittarius - Medium
Capricorn - Low
Aquarius - High
Pisces - Medium

     Libras love luxury, and shower their loved ones in gifts and love. That said, a Libra craves balance in a relationship and will always work to maintain peace. Libras are calm, and they create a relationship that reflects the same. However, Libras often find themselves attracted to people that help them look at life in a new way. For Libras to create balance, they need a partner who helps them grow and evolve in ways they never thought possible.

     So, a Gemini is Libra's perfect match. Libra needs to be challenged and taken out of their comfort zone because that's what they love the most. Geminis are always changing and growing but are willing to learn about their partners. Thus, Gemini and Libra can evolve together; one maintaining peace and the other constantly changing what it means to be peaceful. In contrast, the weakest match for Libra is Capricorn. Libra energy is very calm whereas Capricorn energy is extremely busy. Capricorns love to get to work, while Libras want to take their time and stay relaxed. A Capricorn is often the opposite, in a constant state of stress, which directly conflicts with what Libra wants in life.

A Libra partner will do everything they can to make their loved one happy. Libras jump into relationships quickly because they love to love and be loved. By creating balance in their relationships, Libras thrive on getting pushed out of their comfort zone to new levels of love.

Scorpio

Most compatible Zodiac sign: Cancer
Least compatible Zodiac sign: Gemini

Compatibility Zodiac Sign Ranking for Scorpio:

Aries - High
Taurus - High
Gemini - Low
Cancer - High
Leo - Low
Virgo - High
Libra - Low
Scorpio - Medium
Sagittarius - Low

Capricorn - High
Aquarius - Low
Pisces - High

Scorpios are intense. A Scorpio native will hold on tight to the people in their lives and utilize their watery energy to pay attention to those they love. Scorpios tend to hover and be a little possessive, but they make up for it by being attentive and great listeners. Scorpios are in touch with their emotions, but not outwardly; instead, they are introspective, and work hard to always improve themselves and their relationships.

Because Scorpios are in touch with their emotional sides deeply, that makes Cancers their perfect match. Cancer energy is very supportive when it comes to dating, and Scorpio needs a partner that can understand when they need a mental health day. Scorpio is always working on themselves, and Cancers value someone who is okay with being emotional. That said, Scorpio's least compatible match is Gemini. As you probably know, Geminis have a hard time connecting with people who are in touch with their emotional side. Geminis love to learn, but want to push forward in life; meanwhile, Scorpios tend to stay the same for as long as they can.

Scorpios will love hard; they want to hold on to their relationships forever. A Scorpio native will do their best to make sure that you feel loved, cherished, and accepted in all areas of your life.

Sagittarius

Most compatible Zodiac sign: Aries
Least compatible Zodiac sign: Taurus

Compatibility Zodiac Sign Ranking for Sagittarius:

Aries - High
Taurus - Low
Gemini - Medium
Cancer - Low
Leo - High
Virgo - Low
Libra - Medium
Scorpio - Low
Sagittarius - High
Capricorn - Medium
Aquarius - High
Pisces - Low

Sagittarius people love to have a good time. They are always down for an adventure, and Sagittarius people value partners that will jump at the chance to go with them. Positivity is the name of the Sagittarius game, and they love to be around other people who share in that energy. While Sagittarius natives can be a little hot-headed, they channel that fiery energy into their work and love life as passion and positivity.

No one loves a fire sign quite like a fire sign. Thus, Aries is the perfect match for Sagittarius. These fire signs complement each other because they are both impulsive and adventurous, while also similarly handling their emotions. Sagittarius people want to be positive in all aspects of their lives, which is why Aries compliments them completely. However, Sagittarians are always impulsive and moving to the next thing which makes Taurus their weakest match. Taurus people love to stay in their comfort zone and are not ones for a change, whereas Sagittarius people flourish in the face of change.

Sagittarius people are always down for a good time, but maybe not for a long time. Honor them while they are here, and Sagittarius natives will make the best partners.

Capricorn

Most compatible Zodiac sign: Virgo
Least compatible Zodiac sign: Leo

Compatibility Zodiac Sign Ranking for Capricorn:

Aries - Low
Taurus - High
Gemini - Medium
Cancer - Low
Leo - Low
Virgo - High
Libra - Low
Scorpio - High
Sagittarius - Medium
Capricorn - High
Aquarius - Medium
Pisces - High

Capricorn natives love to work, work, work. They take on new projects every day and find fulfillment in giving their all to something. The same thing applies to Capricorns in relationships; Capricorns love to work alongside their partners and give all they can. However, Capricorn rarely has time to take a break and honor themselves. Thus, they need someone who matches their work ethic but can also implement self-care into their lives.

Enter: Virgo! Virgos complement their fellow earth sign, Capricorn, because they are detail and work-oriented. Virgos pay attention to their partner's needs, which is what Capricorn could always use, but they also thrive on work and taking on new projects. Capricorn and Virgo are almost identical, except Virgo's attention to detail can help Capricorn pay more attention to themselves and what they need. In contrast, Capricorns will not vibe well with vibrant Leo. Leos want to break from routine to go out and play, and they challenge their partners to be confident like them. Capricorn wants to stay out of the limelight, work hard, and isn't one for impulsive adventures.

Hard work and determination is the name of the Capricorn game. If you are looking for someone who can push you to your limits, look no further than a Capricorn. While they can sometimes get lost in their work, they need someone who can remind them to take care of themselves. Maybe that's you!

Aquarius

Most compatible Zodiac signs: Aquarius
Least compatible Zodiac signs: Pisces

Compatibility Zodiac Sign Ranking for Aquarius:

Aries - High
Taurus - Low
Gemini - High
Cancer - Low
Leo - Low
Virgo - Low
Libra - High
Scorpio - Low
Sagittarius - High
Capricorn - Medium
Aquarius - High
Pisces - Low

Aquarius people beat to their drum; they are extremely unique, and they need someone who can match that eclectic nature. Aquarius natives are not emotional, and they value spending time with people who are good listeners and low energy. Aquarius can get overstimulated easily and would rather have quiet nights at home. In a relationship, Aquarius people love to have quality time with their loved one and want to share their unique interests with them.

Aquarius natives vibe the best with other Aquarius people. This is because they are so innately themselves, they need someone who understands why they are the way they are. It can be difficult for Aquarius people to open up right away, and because of that, they need someone who understands that it takes them a long time. In contrast, Pisces have no problem opening up to everyone, everywhere, all of the time. Pisces are emotional and always in dream-like states, which directly contrasts an Aquarian's logical way of thinking. Thus, Pisces and Aquarius can cause each other a lot of frustration when in a relationship.

Aquarius energy is unique per Aquarius individuals. Some are driven, others lazy. Some creative, others plain. Depending on the Aquarius you are dating, you have to understand that they are eccentric in their interests and often completely odd in the best ways.

Pisces

Most compatible Zodiac signs: Taurus
Least compatible Zodiac signs: Aries

Compatibility Zodiac Sign Ranking for Pisces:

Aries - Medium
Taurus - High
Gemini - Low
Cancer - High
Leo - Medium
Virgo - Medium
Libra - Medium
Scorpio - High
Sagittarius - Low
Capricorn - High

Aquarius - Low
Pisces - Medium

Pisces natives are incredibly creative people that often live inside their minds. In a dreamlike state, Pisces are always manifesting their futures. Because of this, Pisces people need someone who is much more grounded in reality and can bring them back to Earth. Pisces can feel insecure sometimes and are prone to anxiety, so having someone patient and kind is the key for this water sign.

It should come as no surprise, then, that Taurus is the perfect match for Pisces energy. Taurus is spiritual, patient, and grounded which is the key to Pisces happiness. Pisces and Taurus pair well because they are like two sides of the same coin, ebbing and flowing. In contrast, Aries energy is the weakest for Pisces. Aries come on strong and are not afraid to tell it how it is. For sensitive Pisces, Aries may be too much energy for them, making them feel unsettled and insecure.

Pisces humans are in love with love, and they will openly give it to those who matter to them. They are creative and always finding ways to be artistic which makes them great gift-givers as well. Pisces can be easily upset, but they find that people who ground them can ultimately inspire radical happiness.

Well, there you have it! If you have been wondering which Zodiac sign is most compatible with yours for dating, we have covered it all. From love languages to compatibility analysis, this section has taken you through it. When looking for a partner, it's important to remember that everyone is different. Just because someone is a Taurus doesn't always mean they are stubborn. If you have learned anything throughout this, it's that you are *so much more than your sun sign*. Everyone is a different makeup of magic that is unique to them, so take astrology with a grain of salt. Astrology especially with dating is a tool/resource for you to better understand yourself and your partner. Use it wisely!

The Return of Saturn (and why it's important)

Thinking about adulthood is probably the farthest thing from your mind, we know. While living in the present is great, astrology can tell you a lot about the entire span of your life. Thus, it can be imperative to learn about how certain planets impact you long term, one of those planets being Saturn.

As you know from previous sections, Saturn is the planet of limitation, a sense of responsibility, and fear. While Saturn is often thought of as depressing or sad, it helps us to see what exactly we are so afraid of and how we can navigate those fears. Whatever limitations you are setting for yourself in life (that maybe you shouldn't be), Saturn can help you to break those limits.

Saturn rules over Capricorn and has naturally masculine energy. A lot of the vibe we get from Saturn is that of a father. Think about your dad setting rules for your family—these rules are limitations on your lifestyle. We don't always like it or agree, but ultimately those rules are for our highest good, set by an authoritative figure. That's what Saturn is all about.

You're probably wondering then *why* Saturn is so important. We didn't give an entire section to all the planets! You're right. Saturn, however, is extremely important in astrology because of your Saturn Return. This sounds scary, but really, you won't have to extensively worry about it for another ten years. But it never hurts to be prepared! Saturn is a planet that teaches us everything we need to learn and improve on. Ultimately, Saturn wants to help us "grow up." Because of that, where our Saturn placement is at birth guides us on our growth journey.

In this section, we're going to break down what a Saturn return is, why it's important, and how it impacts each sign. When looking through the signs (and important dates for each—essentially when your Saturn return is due), cross-reference it with the sign Saturn is in your chart. We will also break down what each sign placement means in Saturn as well.

Let's jump right into it. Here's everything you need to know about Saturn:

First, let's talk about your Saturn return. In astrology, your Saturn return is an astrological transit (meaning that the planet is moving) that happens when Saturn *returns* to the same point in the Zodiac cycle as when you were born.

Saturn will not reach this spot for the first time until you are 29 or 30 years old.

When Saturn returns, it influences your life and is considered to start your "late twenties." What this means is that you are officially an adult! For the first time, you will be met with true adult limitations, challenges, and responsibilities—according to Saturn, anyway. You will start to feel the impact of your Saturn return around the age of 27. Thus, you must know your Saturn sign like the back of your hand, so you can be prepared for whatever lies ahead.

That's where we come in.

We are going to break down each Saturn sign, key dates, and what you can expect from your Saturn now and during your return. That way, you will be ready when your return happens, and can even start taking on the responsibilities Saturn has for you beforehand.

Here are the Saturn return dates for those whose Saturn is in Aries:

Apr 7, 1996, to Jun 9, 1998
Oct 25, 1998, to Feb 28, 1999
May 24, 2025, to Sep 1, 2025
Feb 13, 2026, to Apr 12, 2028

If your Saturn is in Aries, you are extremely resourceful. You are never scared to start over, start fresh, and make the best of what you have. Because of this, you will be able to achieve your goals much faster. Remember, Saturn shows us where our limitations are, including our fears. If your Saturn is in Aries, you probably have issues with confrontation. Decisive action is not your strong suit, and you may avoid conflict as a result. However, you are not egotistical and don't really like asserting yourself. Although, you may find you get defensive when presented with authority.

Some of your life experiences may lead you to become self-centered, which isn't like you. It's okay, though, because you deserve to put yourself first sometimes! As you go through your Saturn return, remember that it is okay to ask for help. People make mistakes, but use yours to learn and grow. You will learn to be self-sufficient, but still, ask for help when you need it! Throughout your process, never stifle yourself. You are passionate and competitive, which are great qualities; never limit yourself to fit into someone else's box. Saturn will remind you of this.

Saturn in Taurus

Here are the Saturn return dates for those whose Saturn is in Taurus:

Jun 9, 1998, to Oct 25, 1998
Feb 28, 1999, to Aug 9, 2000
Oct 15, 2000, to Apr 20, 2001
Apr 12, 2028, to May 31, 2030

Saturn reminds us of what we fear most but also challenges us to break those limitations. With Saturn in Taurus, you fear not having everything you need, loss, change, and being dependent on others. Saturn will highlight these limitations for you, but once you recognize them, you will be able to tackle them one by one. You may feel guilty when you indulge yourself in things you love and have trouble asking for help. Change does not come easy to you, but if you are open to it, everything will begin to work out in your favor.

Your Saturn return will help you to show yourself a little love. You will learn how to celebrate your wins and not feel guilty about them. Likewise, you will develop the skills necessary to ask others for help without feeling like you have failed. You won't be as scared of change, as Saturn will push you into a lot of changes all at once. That's okay—you are strong, and you will be able to tackle each challenge with ease.

Saturn in Gemini

Here are the Saturn return dates for those who have Saturn in Gemini:

Aug 9, 2000, to Oct 15, 2000
Apr 20, 2001, to Jun 3, 2003
May 31, 2030, to Jul 13, 2032

Saturn illuminates what we fear and what our limitations are, which includes things that cause us discomfort. With Saturn in Gemini, you may be uncomfortable expressing yourself; you hide your more eccentric personality from others out of fear you won't be accepted. Often, you are bothered by people who are surface level. If they gossip too much or have a generally negative attitude, you will be standoffish toward them. You fear criticism the most, so you overwork yourself to be perfect in all areas of your life, which can exhaust you completely.

Your Saturn return will help to dismantle all of your fears. You think logically by nature, and that will only grow as you go through your return. Likewise, you make a great teacher and are a great listener. As you move through your Saturn return, you will be reminded to be patient and open-minded to those that enter your life. You will grow into your most authentic self, making you stronger than ever before.

Here are the Saturn return dates for those who have Saturn in Cancer:

Jun 3, 2003, to Jul 16, 2005
Jul 13, 2032, to Aug 26, 2034
Feb 15, 2035, to May 11, 2035

Wherever Saturn falls in your chart indicates what you fear the most and what limits you in life. When Saturn is in Cancer, you may have some limitations in the comfort department. Cancer loves to be nurtured, but Saturn limits that nature—you may feel lonely as if you only have yourself to show comfort. There will be tendencies for you to live in your past; thinking way too hard about things that have hurt you. You will feel uncomfortable when others try to take care of you, even if it's what you truly want deep down. You often are very nurturing to others but don't show that same level of self-care and love to yourself.

When your Saturn return comes through, it will teach you how to love and be loved. You have a hard time accepting when love comes your way, and often find yourself being defensive when someone tries to care for you. When you hit your Saturn return, these boundaries will slowly be broken. With a lot of work, you will mature and gain self-awareness. Through baby steps, you will be able to flip the script and make vulnerability a natural process for you.

Here are the Saturn return dates for those who have Saturn in Leo:

Jul 16, 2005, to Sep 2, 2007
Aug 26, 2034, to Feb 15, 2035
May 11, 2035, to Oct 16, 2036
Feb 11, 2037, to Jul 6, 2037

Remember, Saturn is here to remind us of what our biggest fears and limitations are in life. With Saturn in Leo, you may struggle with your need for attention and approval. When special people enter your life, you meet them with disapproval. Because of this, you may deny your own needs to be the center of attention. You go out of your way when Saturn is in Leo to avoid calling attention to yourself, but then you feel like no one cares about you which causes personal resentment. You may be overly self-conscious and protective of your true self at times. As a result, you put out a false personality that is commandeering and controlling of those around you, because you want to control how others see you.

When your Saturn return happens, be prepared for a shift in your personality. You may find yourself wanting to call attention to yourself, with no regrets. You now will not vibe with people trying to control you, and instead, you will take control of your own life. Leo Saturns are great at making their hobbies into businesses and want to truly shine in the way only Leos can. While it takes a while (until your Saturn return), eventually you will blossom into the strong Lion you

119

were always meant to be, and refuse to care about what other people may think.

Saturn in Virgo

Here are the Saturn return dates for those who have Saturn in Virgo:

Sep 2, 2007, to Oct 29, 2009
Apr 7, 2010, to Jul 21, 2010
Oct 16, 2036, to Feb 11, 2037
Jul 6, 2037, to Sep 5, 2039

Saturn tells us, in a not-so-subtle way, what our limitations are. With Saturn in Virgo, you will feel limited by routine, work, and your keen attention to detail. While these sound like good things, they can block you from living your best life. You may find that you identify with the phrase "overworked and underpaid." The key to breaking out of this cycle is finding joy in what you do—from routine to work to even your home life. However, you may find that you struggle with this for quite a while.

Lucky for you, Virgo Saturn, is that you will eventually find joy in all areas of your life. When you hit your Saturn return, you will be presented with intense changes that alter the way you think about things. Work won't seem so daunting, and you will learn to appreciate the little things in life. You will channel that eye for detail into things that spark joy, while you leave everything else in your dust. Self-honesty will be the best way to tackle your problems, as it will help provide you with clarity on what it is that you want out of life. You deserve it!

Saturn in Libra

Here are the Saturn return dates for those with Saturn in Libra:

Oct 29, 2009, to Apr 7, 2010
Jul 21, 2010, to Oct 5, 2012
Sep 5, 2039, to Nov 11, 2041
Jun 21, 2042, to Jul 14, 2042

Saturn reminds us of what our fears and limitations are and helps us to grow through and move past them. With a Saturn in Libra, you crave balance and stability. However, with balance comes weighing both sides of every situation heavily against each other. As a result, you may struggle with making decisions properly because you can see both sides. Every option will weigh on you and ultimately limit you from being successful in that way.

Your sense of love for others is strong; you want to please everyone and have them be happy all the time. Thus, you like to jump to the part of the relationship that is comfortable and stay there for the rest of your days. Your Saturn return will have you break this cycle to pieces. As a result, you will find confidence in making decisions and help to become a leader in your pack. As you change and transform, your friendships will begin to feel more genuine and will last for much longer. You are allowed to be confident; embrace it!

Here are the Saturn return dates for those who have Saturn in Scorpio:

Oct 5, 2012, to Dec 23, 2014
Jun 14, 2015, to Sep 17, 2015
Nov 11, 2041, to Jun 21, 2042
Jul 14, 2042, to Feb 21, 2044
Mar 25, 2044, to Oct 31, 2044

Saturn looks at what our deepest limitations and fears are and bubbles them up to the surface to confront head-on. Thus, Scorpio Saturns may feel a little unstable because they want nothing but to bottle everything up inside. If your Saturn is in Scorpio, you may have trouble expressing some of your emotions; the emotions you consider to be "bad" will hold you back from your fullest potential. For example, Scorpio Saturns do not like to confront their jealous or possessive nature, and they bottle that up until they feel like they are going to explode. Being openly vulnerable is not Scorpio Saturn's strong suit. Scorpio Saturns are extremely ambitious, almost to a fault, and they can be untrusting of others when they feel someone is keeping a secret from them.

However, during your Saturn return, you may find yourself opening up to others in ways you never have before. It will be challenging, as you are stepping out of your comfort zone to do something that may frighten you. Remember, Saturn loves for you to confront what you fear. As you become more open to vulnerability, you will notice that your entire personality begins to soften. Your walls will come down, and you will find joy in talking through things with your loved ones, perhaps for the first time in your entire life. Scorpio Saturn, you have your work cut out for you, but it will be so worth it. Scorpio Saturns can use their inner power of transformation with the same will that drives their ambition.

Saturn in Sagittarius

Here are the Saturn return dates for those who have Saturn in Sagittarius:

Dec 23, 2014, to Jun 14, 2015
Sep 17, 2015, to Dec 19, 2017
Feb 21, 2044, to Mar 25, 2044
Oct 31, 2044, to Jan 24, 2047
Jul 10, 2047, to Oct 22, 2047

Saturn reminds us that our fears and limitations are not worth our energy, and it encourages us to face them directly. As a Sagittarius Saturn, you will have very little patience. You don't like to hear embellishments and would rather people get straight to the point. There's no time like the present, and you don't want to waste a minute of it. Sagittarius Saturns like to play by their own rules, and if put into a box, they will feel extremely uncomfortable. You don't like to step out of your mental comfort zone, whatever that may look like for you, and fear becoming the same as others around you.

When your Saturn return comes to play, you will find that you are being challenged in totally new ways. Saturn in Sagittarius wants to set some rules and boundaries in your life, which you will not be receptive to at first. However, as you are an adult once your return happens, it is time to face the facts. It's time for you to come back down to Earth and settle down for a little while. Find a balance between adventure and security, and remind yourself that you are worth it. Nothing can stop you now!

Saturn in Capricorn

Here are the Saturn return dates for those with Saturn in Capricorn:

Dec 19, 2017, to Mar 21, 2020
Jul 1, 2020, to Dec 17, 2020
Jan 24, 2047, to Jul 10, 2047
Oct 22, 2047, to Jan 21, 2050

Saturn is here to remind you that your fears and limitations will never make you who you are. For Saturn in Capricorn, you will be headstrong and self-reliant. Why work with others when you can do the best job yourself? You may find you tend to overwork yourself in that regard because you truly believe you are the best one for the job. While you have strong desires for success, you fear rejection and force yourself to over-perfect your work at all times. Thus, your workaholic tendencies are your biggest limitations because they are rooted in fear. Capricorn Saturns are very rule-oriented and want to do everything the "right" way.

When your Saturn return happens, you will be met with one of the biggest decisions of your life. You can either continue down the path of exhaustion or enter a new phase of your life that is a lot slower paced. Saturn in Capricorn thrives on common sense and thinks logically through every decision they make. As a result, you will come to the right choice as it pertains to your lifestyle. Saturn returns help to eliminate or evolve our limitations into something that serves our highest good. Because of this, you will be able to thrive and prosper, if you allow yourself the courtesy. You can do this!

Saturn in Aquarius

Here are the Saturn return dates for those with Saturn in Aquarius:

Feb 6, 1991, to May 21, 1993
Jun 30, 1993, to Jan 28, 1994
Mar 21, 2020, to Jul 1, 2020
Dec 17, 2020, to Mar 7, 2023

Saturn highlights what our deepest fears are, how they limit us, and how to push through them. With Saturn in Aquarius, you will be able to think realistically about pretty much everything. Your friends will value the logic you present in each conversation, and you can be extremely decisive. Thus, you have an easy time making friends; especially friends that are older than you. However, you struggle deeply with leaving your comfort zone socially and when you meet someone who is not your standard type of friend, you tend to shy away. You are a natural-born leader, and as such, you drive people to you. However, you get exhausted easily from the social activity and will pull away.

Throughout your Saturn return, you will be challenged in ways you probably wouldn't expect. Saturn in Aquarius values stability when it comes to relationships, and you mate for life (as they say). Your Saturn return will have people abruptly leave your life for seemingly no reason, which will shock you to your core. However, this is Saturn's way of opening space in your life for new people that are way outside your norm. Embrace them, embrace the change, and watch yourself transform into a social butterfly. You can do this!

Saturn in Pisces

Here are the Saturn return dates for those with Saturn in Pisces:

May 21, 1993, to Jun 30, 1993
Jan 28, 1994, to Apr 7, 1996
Mar 7, 2023, to May 24, 2025
Sep 1, 2025, to Feb 13, 2026

Saturn looks at what limits you in life, forces you to tackle those fears, and brings you the happiest version of yourself possible. For Pisces Saturns, there can be a lot of confusion going on in your life. While you are an emotional person, you find excessive shows of feelings, emotions, or vulnerability to be quite uncomfortable. Thus, when it comes time to interact with others and open up, you have a hard time expressing exactly what it is that you want to convey.

Pisces usually find vulnerability to be easy, but not within a Saturn placement. As a result, they can be too introspective and self-sacrificing.

During your Saturn return, you will be presented with new relationships. Throughout these relationships, you will find that you have the chance to be truly vulnerable. Here, Pisces Saturns will have to choose if they want to open up to their new friends or become closed off. Saturn will force you to be excessively emotional and vulnerable in a way that you can't control, which releases your fears and anxieties. Once you move through your Saturn return, you will find that you can open up with ease and find a new comfortable lifestyle for yourself within your friendships.

Now that you know what your Saturn return is going to look like, let's talk a little bit about what's going on realistically.

Your Saturn return marks your passage into "real adulthood," as you know, and happens roughly around 29.5 years of age. You may be thinking, does that mean we have a Saturn return every 29.5ish years? The short answer is: yes. However, are you ready for your mind to be blown?

Your Saturn return happens when you are entering new phases of your life. The first Saturn return is referred to as your quarter-life crisis, and you can feel the impact of it starting around age 25. You guessed it, your second Saturn return is your *mid-life crisis*. Your parents may be going through this now! It's a time where you are reminded how short life is and crave to be young once again. Saturn releases you of your fears and limitations and helps you to be your happiest self. Thus, when people hit their second Saturn return, they start to do some outlandish things in the name of "being old." While sometimes silly, getting older is a wonderful thing, and they deserve to live a little.

Hopefully, now you have a better understanding of Saturn and how the planet works to aid in your life path direction. Your Saturn return will be a doozy, but now you are prepared! We can't talk about astrology pathways without talking about Saturn, despite you being a teenager. You want to have this knowledge early, so you can be ready. Furthermore, you now know what your biggest fears and limitations are, and you can get to work on breaking down those barriers ahead of time. Look at you go!

Next, we will be chatting about all things Mercury Retrograde. Also known as the time each year where communication is terrible, the technology always fails, and your exes somehow make their way back into your life again. Are you ready for the ride?

What's the Deal with Mercury Retrograde, Anyway?

If you know anything about astrology, you have probably heard about Mercury retrograde. Mercury retrograde is infamous for causing all sorts of personal chaos. But what does Mercury retrograde really mean, anyway?

We have talked a little about Mercury retrograde already, but as a refresher: when a planet is retrograde it gives the appearance of spinning backward. Imagine this as the planet working the opposite of how it's supposed to. All the planets have a retrograde period, not just good old Mercury; however, Mercury retrograde happens often and has an extremely strong impact on us. Think about Mercury Rx (retrograde shorthand) like this: Mercury is the planet of communication, and when it's working backward, it complicates how we communicate with one another. How do we communicate in 2021? Through technology, of course.

Mercury retrograde usually lasts about three weeks to one month. However, there are two "shadow periods" when it comes to planets in retrograde. These shadow periods happen before and after a planet goes retrograde. Thus, when Mercury goes retrograde the shadow period will occur right before and right after; usually, the shadow period is a week before and lasts a week or two after Mercury retrograde. The shadow period means that before a planet goes retrograde, you will already be feeling the effects of it. Likewise, you will continue to feel the effects after the planet retrogrades, too. This can be a good thing! Shadow periods help us prepare for a transition, moving into a retrograde, and leaving it.

In this section, we will walk you through how Mercury retrograde impacts each Zodiac sign (which can be applied to that sign in Mercury as well) and some dos and don'ts when it comes to the retrograde period. Likewise, there's a lot to take in when it comes to Mercury Rx, and we will cover it all. That way, when you experience a Mercury Rx, you will be ready to have your defenses up and combat its impact. Without further ado, let's jump right into it.

First things first, let's talk about Mercury itself. Mercury is our planet of communication, as you know. When you look at what sign your Mercury is in, you begin to understand how you download information from other people, how you interact, and what you put out there yourself. When Mercury is retrograde, suddenly everything you just learned about yourself flies out the window. Don't be scared! We are going to help you learn how to navigate through this process. What's great about Mercury retrograde is that it affects everyone in similar ways.

Here are some things to look out for during Mercury Rx in particular:

Technology will fail you. Technology deciding it doesn't want to work is one constant with Mercury Rx. Mercury Rx is trying to eliminate the most effective forms of communication and interferes with the way we utilize tech.

For example, Wi-Fi will crash, your Word doc won't save properly, or cell service will drop as soon as your friend answers the phone. Trust no iPhone during Mercury retrograde!

You will have communication slip-ups. Especially in the world we live in, it's nearly impossible to escape that text message typo. Expect to not be able to type properly when it comes to conversation and have everything you say misunderstood. It's just part of what makes Mercury retrograde so much fun.

Big decisions will be twice as hard. When it comes to Mercury retrograde, it is not always the best time to make big choices in your life. Moving will be twice as hard, and accepting a new job won't be as easy as it could be. This is because our communication and tech are failing! Imagine starting a new job and your email login won't work, or moving to a new home and losing the house keys. While you may not be moving or working as a teenager, you still have big choices to make in your life; see if you can't push them off by a month. If that's not possible, take as much time as you can to prepare yourself.

Traveling becomes incredibly challenging. Family vacations are one of the most difficult things to do that eventually lead to blessings. If you are vacationing during Mercury Rx, think about how you communicate with your family. GPS will fail, hotel keys won't work, gas will run out, and other critical things will fail. If you can make it through traveling during Mercury retrograde, more power to you, as fighting is almost inevitable.

Now that you know what to look out for in a broader sense, we can tackle the dos and don'ts of Mercury retrograde per your Zodiac sign. These can be applied to your Mercury sign as well (for example, Pisces Mercury will have similar traits to what we are about to list out for Pisces as a whole). There may be some differences depending on placement, of course, but the vibes will be similar. Here's how we'll break it down:

Your Zodiac Sign + How Mercury Retrograde Impacts It + Dos and Don'ts During Mercury Retrograde for That Zodiac Sign

Ready to jump right in? Let's do it.

Aries during Mercury Retrograde: Aries love to get things done. Most of the time, Aries are ready to go full speed ahead; they are problem solvers, natural-born leaders, and are ready for anything. That said, during Mercury retrograde, Aries will be confronted with several roadblocks on their way. Patience will be required from Aries whenever Mercury is retrograde because they won't be able to reach their destinations right away. This may cause Aries to become frustrated and angry, especially because restraint is not their strong suit.

Aries Mercury Rx Dos: Keep pushing, but implement patience into your routine.

Aries Mercury Rx Don'ts: Don't let anger get the best of you; impatience will be your downfall.

Taurus during Mercury Retrograde: Tauruses are naturally calm and grounded people. However, during Mercury retrograde, Taurus's calm energy will be challenged as every single little thing begins going wrong. Taurus may find themselves making impulsive decisions as a result, which will throw them off balance a little as they are not used to impulsivity. A Taurus likes to think rationally, but Mercury retrograde will try its hardest not to allow them to. Thus, Taurus may feel a little less stable during these times of the year.

Taurus Mercury Retrograde Dos: Keep trying to maintain your balance and composure. Don't let Mercury retrograde get you down.

Taurus Mercury Retrograde Don'ts: Avoid blaming other people, and don't be too hard on those around you. They are going through it, too.

Gemini during Mercury Retrograde: Gemini is ruled by Mercury, so as you can imagine, Mercury operating backward can tussle Gemini's life. Gemini loves to learn and take on new projects but may find that Mercury retrograde causes them to feel lazy. Mercury retrograde will challenge Gemini to find new routes to reach their goals, but Gemini may feel like they are rushing forward to go nowhere. If Gemini slows down a little, they may find that they can conquer Mercury retrograde all on their own.

Gemini Mercury Retrograde Dos: Slow down. Give yourself a chance to breathe and figure out how to tackle your newfound goals and aspirations.

Gemini Mercury Retrograde Don'ts: Don't fret too much when social media apps are down and communication is rough. You've got this.

Cancer during Mercury Retrograde: Cancers feel everything on a deeper level than the other Zodiac signs. Thus, when Mercury is retrograde, Cancers tend to go back into their shells because of all the information (or misinformation) they receive. Cancers will find that their moods are unstable and constantly shifting during Mercury retrograde. When things start to spiral out of control, Cancer will find that they have a hard time bouncing back. Mercury retrograde is a trying time for Cancers.

Cancer Mercury Retrograde Dos: Be gentle with yourself during this time. Softness and self-care will be imperative to move forward out of Mercury retrograde.

Cancer Mercury Retrograde Don'ts: Don't retreat into your shell too much if you can help it. You will get through this, believe it.

Leo during Mercury Retrograde: Leos, by nature, love to be in the spotlight. Being the center of attention comes naturally to Leo placements, but their biggest fears also lie there too. Leos get uncomfortable when something goes wrong when they are at the center of it, and Mercury retrograde will cause just about everything to go wrong. Thus, Leo may feel a little unhinged during this time, as everything seems to be failing and out of their control; possibly reflecting poorly on them, as well. Mercury retrograde can be difficult to navigate for these sunny, happy Leos.

Leo Mercury Retrograde Dos: Take a step back when things go wrong and remember this is not about you—you are amazing, and sometimes things can get out of control. It's okay!

Leo Mercury Retrograde Don'ts: Don't take your frustration out on other people, as they are going through it too. Remember that you can do this!

Virgo during Mercury Retrograde: Virgo is also ruled by Mercury, which means that retrograde can throw them completely out of whack. Virgo craves structure and order, and Mercury retrograde deprives them of all of that. Virgos want to analyze everything and have things completely perfect so that they can stick to their routines, but Mercury will challenge everything they thought they knew during retrograde. Because of this, Virgos must tap into the side of them that is rooted, grounded, and chill (as an earth sign this should come naturally). Once they do that, Virgo can push through retrograde with ease.

Virgo Mercury Retrograde Dos: Tap into your calm side and find ways to channel your panic into productive projects.

Virgo Mercury Retrograde Don'ts: Don't panic, and don't wallow in your panic. Don't let retrograde get the best of you, Virgo!

Libra during Mercury Retrograde: Libras value their friendships and other relationships possibly more than anything else in their lives. As a result, when Mercury retrograde screws up communication, Libras can have a difficult time adjusting. Their relationships will become strained, and this can cause Libra to have a bit of an identity crisis. Likewise, people from their past tend to pop back up, wanting to reconnect. This will be a challenging time for Libras to navigate, but they always come out on the other side better for it.

Libra Mercury Dos: Do try to remain calm when communication goes haywire, and be open to new connections in their place.

Libra Mercury Don'ts: Don't act out of frustration or anger, as it is not your strong suit. Don't cause imbalance.

Scorpio during Mercury Retrograde: Scorpios are not the type of people to crave adventure or action in their lives. When Mercury retrograde comes to play, Scorpio may begin to feel uncomfortable and act out of panic. However, Scorpio can usually handle Mercury Rx pretty well, because they know that there is an end in sight. So, even when hardship is thrown their way, Scorpios will push through it, looking ahead instead of in the past. They just need to get through that initial stress and panic, and then they are home free.

Scorpio Mercury Retrograde Dos: Do allow yourself some grace and time for self-care.

Scorpio Mercury Retrograde Don'ts: Don't allow the panic to become your identity. Instead, channel it into calmness and work on you. It's going to be okay!

Sagittarius during Mercury Retrograde: Sagittarius people are always on the go; they thrive when their life is non-stop and love to be busy. Mercury retrograde, however, will put an immediate halt in a Sag's lifestyle. When technology stops working and people don't communicate well, Sagittarius is forced to slow down and stop what they are doing. Thus, Mercury retrograde can throw Sagittarius for a loop, and they may find that during this time they are extremely uncomfortable and unhappy. Although, slowing down usually does a Sagittarius a lot of good, after the fact.

Sagittarius Mercury Retrograde Dos: Do react calmly when you need to slow down; show yourself a little self-care during this time.

Sagittarius Mercury Retrograde Don'ts: Don't overreact or take your frustration out on others. You can do this!

Capricorn during Mercury Retrograde: Capricorns have work to do, and often don't like to rely on anyone else to get it done. As a result, Mercury retrograde will toss everything Capricorn holds dear to the side. Capricorns will now have to talk with other people to get help making their technology work, and they will have to deal with things slowing down a little bit. A slower pace isn't usually Cap's style, but Mercury Rx will be testing them to develop some slower habits. They want to be in control, but Capricorn will have to learn that sometimes letting others in is okay and can even be helpful in the long run.

Capricorn Mercury Retrograde Dos: Do remain calm when things slow down a bit. It may even be good for you!

Capricorn Mercury Retrograde Don'ts: Don't be scared to ask other people for help. That's what they are there for!

Aquarius during Mercury Retrograde: Aquarius people have an affinity for technology and invention, so when Mercury goes retrograde, it can cause a lot of frustration for them. Technology will refuse to work correctly, and it can become a chore to fix your gadgets over and over...and over. Never fear, Aquarius is the person for the job, but they may find themselves a little overwhelmed at how much needs to be done. That's okay—Mercury Rx will remind Aquarius that it's okay to take breaks from time to time, and not all technology has to work perfectly all of the time.

Aquarius Mercury Retrograde Dos: Do fix things as needed, and take some time to enjoy the slower-paced lifestyle that Mercury Rx is bringing.

Aquarius Mercury Retrograde Don'ts: Don't freak out and get overly frustrated. Remember that things always work out in the end.

Pisces during Mercury Retrograde: Pisces will find that Mercury retrograde is not the worst thing ever for them. Pisces live in their worlds and often have trouble communicating anyway, and they are not often consumed with technology. However, the conflict will arise when others have communication issues with Pisces. This causes anxiety for Pisces and frustration as they can't access the Internet as easily to research how to resolve the issue. Pisces are extremely empathic and often impacted by those around them, making their Mercury retrograde experience slightly frustrating.

Pisces Mercury Retrograde Dos: Do keep doing your own thing and try not to worry too much about what others think.

Pisces Mercury Retrograde Don'ts: Don't let yourself get overwhelmed, and go with the flow instead.

Hopefully, you now have a better sense of what Mercury retrograde is and how it impacts your chart. You can always reference each sign of your big three here and your Mercury sign to delve into how Merc Rx will impact you in different ways. Things can become wonky during the times Mercury enters into retrograde, but remember that there is always an upside to these challenges. Once you start to notice how Retrograde affects you, you can find ways to push through it and make it gentler. You've got this, promise!

Now it's time to jump back into those Zodiac signs and explain them a little more in-depth since you have a basic understanding of how it all works. Are you down? Let's do it.

Conclusion

You have probably heard your English teacher say never to start your conclusion off with "In conclusion..." so we aren't! See what we did there? Jokes aside, it's that time where we talk about everything you have learned and how you can take it with you in your daily life.

We have talked about all twelve of the Zodiac signs, their elements, their modalities, and how they work within your chart. Each part of your natal chart tells you a little bit about the blend of magic that makes you who you are. When you begin to put those pieces together, you will quickly learn how you interact with the world around you and the thoughts within you. Likewise, you will also be able to perceive others in your life—from dating to your relationships with your parents, astrology covers it all.

You have also learned a lot about the planets and how they impact you. From your Saturn Return to Mercury Retrograde, there has been a lot of deep diving into your planets. Thus, you understand how each Zodiac sign is ruled by each planet, and what that means for you and those around you. It's fun stuff, truly.

But wait! There's more!

We don't want to leave you hanging—we are also going to provide you with some other astrology resources so you can continue your education on the topic. We obviously can't cover everything here, and in astrology, you can always learn more because it is so complex. So, we are going to give you additional resources to delve into and learn more. Likewise, booking a Natal Chart reading with a professional Astrologer can help you to learn even more about your chart (and you, by design).

Thank you for joining us on this astrology journey! We hope that you have learned a lot about the Cosmos, and we are thrilled for you to continue that education down the road!

Astrology Resources

Horos - Horos is an astrology app for your phone. In it, you can enter your chart info as well as friends and family (which will break down compatibility as well).

Daily Horoscope - Another astrology app, but will be your daily horoscope! Read horoscopes for your "Big Three" to get a deeper sense of what the universe is telling you.

Cafe Astrology - Cafe Astrology is a great website with tons of astrology information. Likewise, you can look up your chart for free on Cafe Astrology as well.

Horoscope.com is another great online resource for anything related to horoscopes.

The Only Astrology Book You'll Ever Need - This book is quite literally the only astrology book you'll ever need, as it covers everything under the sun (and in the cosmos) you will need to reference.

What's Your Sign Podcast - What's Your Sign is a great podcast that delves into specifics on astrology, one episode at a time.

Moon Matters Pod - Another great podcast for all things astrology!

Nourished Natasha Yoga - Natasha is a Yoga Teacher on YouTube that tailors her (free) online classes to what is going on astrologically in the year. Definitely great if you are into yoga!

Made in the USA
Middletown, DE
12 December 2021